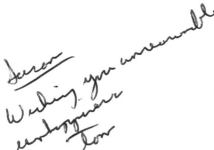

TESTIMC

MAKING LIFE WORK includes some excellent positive and anti-disturbing philosophy that can help the reader enjoy a distinctly less self-defeating life. Much straight thinking!

Albert Ellis, Ph. D.
President, Albert Ellis Institute, New York
Author of *A Guide to Rational Living*

A fine and beautifully written book. Full of deep wisdom, and the sense of being guided by someone who cares. MAKING LIFE WORK is a map for navigating life's most difficult challenges. But it's far more. It sounds clear and eloquent warnings about the psychological traps that destroy happiness, and shows exactly what to do to overcome them. Highly recommended for anyone who seeks the skills and wisdom to build a better life.

Matthew McKay, Ph.D.
Author of *Self Esteem*

An inspiring testimonial to the human spirit.

Helen Klein
UltraRunner's Hall of Fame

www.drzinkle.com

Making Life Work

The Struggle for Psychological Health

by

Tom Zinkle, Ph.D.

Bridgewood Press
Phoenix, Arizona

Acknowledgements

Sincere appreciation to the following individuals who read my manuscript and provided constructive criticism that greatly improved the work: Laura Abood, Ph. D.; Ann C. Batiza; M. Joseph Cosgrove, M. D.; Jeanie Gerstein; Susan McClure, LISW; Donna Robberecht, LCSW; Jennifer Salib, Psy.D., and Joseph Yakira, M. D.

I owe even greater appreciation to the following individuals who provided feedback regarding content and/or literary technique: Jed Davis; Gary Fell, Ph. D.; and Craig Gotsill.

Above all I thank my beautiful and feisty wife Norma (the only person I insist call me "doctor") who supported me throughout the most difficult and demanding process I have ever undertaken.

© 2004, Tom Zinkle, Ph.D.
All rights reserved.   www.drzinkle.com

Cover graphics by Cortney Bell
Photograph by Catherine Connell

Library of Congress Cataloging-in-Publication Data

Zinkle, Tom, 1944-
    Making life work: the struggle for psychological health / by
    Tom Zinkle.
        p. cm.
    Includes bibliographical references.
    ISBN 0-927015-24-2 (trade pbk. : alk.paper)
    1. Conduct of life. I. Title

    BF637.C5Z56 2004
    158—dc22

                                    2004022962

Printed in the United States of America

Table of Contents

Introduction

Living life well is neither easy nor common; it requires extraordinary courage, wisdom, and common sense. Freud was so unimpressed with our ability to live sensibly that he postulated that people have a death instinct — a compelling sub-conscious need to hurt themselves and eventually lead to their own demise and death. I joke with clients that we should get two lives—one to learn how to live and then one to do it. Many of us who reflect back on our life in later years wish we had known earlier what we know now; we wish we could turn back the hands of time and start life over.

Even if we can't undo what's done, can't do what went undone, can't recover wasted years, hopefully we at least learn from experience. In 30 years as a practicing psychologist, I have had the opportunity to learn not only from my own mistakes and successes but also from the mistakes and successes of the estimated 8,000 clients I have worked with in therapy—all seeking greater satisfaction and happiness, all searching for ways, however miraculously or straightforward and simple, to make life work. Over the years I developed basic themes and key ideas for dealing effectively with life and life's problems. In an attempt to summarize these themes and ideas, I undertook the writing of this book.

Influenced by my Wisconsin farm background, I cherish common sense. Deceased therapy expert Milton Erickson, M. D. who also grew up on a farm in Wisconsin, once commented, "If you wake up in the morning, put your pants on." While drawing heavily upon my training and experience as a psychologist, and my fascination with Eastern thought, this book is anything but technical or theoretical. It is obsessed with living with courage and wisdom, all the while not forgetting to put one's pants on. It stresses the importance of living with intensity and passion rather than hiding from life out of neurotic fear. It stresses the value of hard work and perseverance; not being afraid of failure or what others might think; having goals, interests, and meaningful relationships. Specific techniques are offered for living with peace and tranquility, developing healthy self-esteem, over-coming fear and anxiety, overcoming procrastination, preventing depression, letting go of anger, and having a successful and happy marriage.

Some people are more afraid of life than committed to living fully. Much of their energy is spent judging themselves and being concerned with what others think of them. They resist life and feel victimized. Their life becomes a constant protest that people shouldn't do what they do, that life shouldn't be the way it is, that things that happen shouldn't happen. They are too preoccupied with fear of the future, regret about the past, and resistance to what is, to take advantage of the wonderful gift of life and the opportunities life offers. They make life infinitely more difficult than it needs to be and experience little lasting happiness and tranquility.

In contrast to the misery experienced by neurotic individuals as they fear the future and lament the past, psychologically healthy people experience profound peace and tranquility as they live intensely dedicated to the present. They are more concerned with living than worried about their own worth or what others think of them. They attempt to make life what they want rather than seeing themselves as helpless victims of fate; but they have a profound ability and willingness to accept what then happens. They don't fear what might happen; they don't experience anger, depression, or self-pity over what does happen—even when that is not what they wanted or attempted to make happen. They understand and live the proverbial wisdom that: "You cannot attain happiness; when you surrender all the conditions you think you need to be happy, happiness attains you."

Some of the themes and key ideas for living effectively seem so obvious and straightforward as to belie their importance and profundity. They seem little more than common sense; and, at first glance, it is surprising that everyone does not practice them routinely. Unfortunately, as we all discover in observing those around us, and too often in our own life, "common sense is not all that common." These "obvious" lessons in wisdom include:

1. Courage isn't the absence of fear, but the willingness to act despite fear.
2. Psychologically healthy people cherish life but are not afraid of death. Death is not as sad as the fact that many people never really live and many people live in vulgar obscene ways.
3. People without goals, interests, and meaningful relationships are significantly more susceptible to depression than their counterparts.
4. Life works as well as a person's biggest flaw.
5. Marriage demands and depends on love.

Marital problems develop and escalate not so much because of communication problems but because love isn't easy.

Other lessons in wisdom are counter-intuitive and anything but obvious. Often the only way of making progress against life's common headwinds is to plot a non-direct, zigzag course. These lessons are unlikely to be discovered without assistance or considerable life experience; and even when discovered, are prone to be forgotten or abandoned for approaches that intuitively seem more natural. These counter-intuitive lessons in wisdom include:

1. Anyone can be happy when he gets what he wants; it takes a truly healthy person to be happy regardless, without any reason whatsoever. That is what true mental health is all about.
2. The way to develop a better sense of self is to be less focused on self and more focused on life and being part of the human family. This circumvents the problems connected to self-evaluation and leads to being a psychologically healthier, more mature person.
3. There's something illogical about looking for easy ways to accomplish difficult tasks. Psychologically healthy people are turned on by challenge and difficulty rather than overwhelmed with fear or denial.
4. Doing is often more important than doing perfectly. Few things need to be done perfectly and many things worth doing are worth doing poorly.
5. The more someone accepts their partner as they are, the more likely their partner is to change.
6. A person's greatest asset, out of balance, can

become his greatest failing.

The following sources of wisdom (from different eras, different cultures and traditions, and different life perspectives) have influenced me throughout my now too many years; in that regard, and for any wisdom presented in this book, I am indebted to:

1. The clients I have worked with in therapy. I hope they have learned as much from me as I have learned from them.
2. Western psychology in general, and in particular:
   (a) Karen Horney, M. D. who reshaped psycho-analytic theory into modern day relevance.
   (b) Psychiatrist Milton Erickson, M. D.
   (c) Albert Ellis, Ph. D. the psychologist who developed Rational Emotive Behavior Therapy.
3. Eastern thought in general, and in particular:
   (a) Peaceful Warrior and author Dan Millman.
   (b) Sufism: the mystical branch of Islam.
   (c) Spiritualist Eckhart Tolle.
   (d) The work of Japanese psychiatrist Shoma Morita, M. D. based upon Buddhist principles, as presented by David Reynolds.
4. Inspirational author Og Mandino.

Life doesn't have to be as difficult as we make it. In the process of living, we become psychologically healthier or more neurotic; we acquire greater wisdom or repeat the same mistakes over and over. The healthier and wiser we become the easier life is; the more neurotic and unenlightened we become the more impossible life becomes. This is a book of great hope; it attempts to uncover the hidden obstacles along life's journey so that life can be lived with prevailing tranquility and happiness. I write this book in the hope that it may inspire courage and provide wisdom beyond your years so that you might live with greater effectiveness and satisfaction.

Chapter ONE
THE ART OF BEING UNREASONABLY HAPPY

There is nothing wrong with intellectual understanding.
But it need not be pursued at the expense of missing
the experience of tasting one's salad.
David Reynolds [1]

It can be fun to watch cats or dogs—they seem to live spontaneously and in an uncomplicated manner. In contrast humans have too much noise going on in their head: What if it rains? What will happen when I get there? What will others think of me? How do I look? How could I be so stupid? As part of being in their head, people commonly are not in the present. Driving to work, they think about what they will do when they get there. At work they think about what they will have for dinner or about tomorrow's meeting. It's like the joke: "While making love to his wife, he thinks about work; at work he thinks about making love to his wife." It would be shocking to most people to realize how little time they spend focused on the present.

Being in one's head, rather than in the present, lends itself to resisting rather than accepting and experiencing reality as it is. Resisting reality is the essence of neurotic disturbance—including anxiety, depression, and anger. Before exploring these issues, allow me to highlight the benefit to be gained. Some people are at peace with life—having little fear, anger, depression, self-pity, guilt. They experience great joy and happiness. To be one of this select group, you need to understand and put into practice two interconnected qualities—living in the present and accepting reality as it is. Dr. Wayne Dyer describes such people:

> *First and most obviously, you see people who like virtually everything about life—people who are comfortable doing just about anything, and who waste no time in complaining, or wishing that things were otherwise. They are enthusiastic about life, and they want all that they can get out of it. They like picnics, movies, books, sports, concerts, cities, farms, animals, mountains and just about everything. They like life. When you are around people like this you'll note an absence of grumbling, moaning, or even passive sighing. If it rains, they like it. If it's hot, they dig it, rather than complain about it. If they are in a traffic jam, or at a party, or all alone, they simply deal with what is there. There is no pretending to enjoy, but a sensible acceptance of what is, and an outlandish ability to delight in that reality. Ask them what they don't like and they are hard pressed to come up with an honest answer. They don't have sense enough to come in out of the rain, because they see rain as beautiful, thrilling and something to experience. They like it. Slush doesn't send them into a fury; they observe it, splash around in it, and accept it as part of what it means to be alive. Do they like cats? Yes. Bears? Yes. Worms? Yes. While such annoyances as disease, droughts, mosquitoes, floods and the like are not warmly embraced*

by such people, they never spend any of their present moments complaining about them, or wishing that they weren't so. If situations need to be eradicated, they will work at eradicating them—and enjoy the work. Try as you might, you'll have a tough time coming up with something they'll dislike doing. Truly, they are likers of life, and they wallow in all of it, getting out of it all that is possible for them. [2]

Our mind is meant to help us, but it can be our worst enemy. Obsessive-Compulsive Disorder is an anxiety disorder that exhibits this problem to the extreme; for such people it's as if their mind has turned against them—they drive themselves crazy with thoughts they can neither control nor stop. Their mind tortures them with the scariest or most disgusting thoughts it can come up with, even though these thoughts have no basis in reality. Maybe they left the stove on—even though they have already checked it a dozen times. I saw one man obsessed with the thought that he might stab his 4-year-old daughter, even though he would die before he would harm this daughter. I recently saw a neonatal nurse obsessed with the idea that she might hold a newborn baby too tight and thus seriously injure it. Frequent themes for obsessive people are that they are evil, homosexual, sexually inadequate, or just inadequate in general; that they have done or will do something terrible; or that something terrible will happen. I saw one client obsessed with the thought that his penis was visually deformed; he literally would have to go into the restroom frequently to reassure himself this wasn't the case. Woody Allen movies frequently portray characters obsessed with their own inadequacy; Woody once said he was going to give his psychiatrist one more year, and then he was going to Lourdes. For such people, it's like it would take a miracle to escape from their own mind.

Most anxiety is connected to being in one's head rather than in the present. Some people worry so much about what might happen in the future that they hardly experience what is happening here and now. The term "anticipatory anxiety" describes the anxiety that develops when people worry about the future rather than live in the present. Anxiety involves resistance to what might happen. In depression and anger, people resist what has happened and thus what is; they get depressed or angry about what happened or didn't happen instead of accepting and experiencing reality as it is. All neurotic emotion is an internal process of resisting life, what has happened or might happen, rather than experiencing reality in the present moment and the peace and tranquility that potentially accompanies that experience.

People have pronounced problems being in their head rather than in the present—even if not to the extent of these neurotic disorders. They are unaware of the constant dialogue that goes on in their head. If you live in New York City long enough, you don't notice the noise; but come back from a two-week vacation in Hawaii, and it will be deafening. Herbert Benson, M.D. [3] concluded that our minds need not race as they usually do, that people can learn to produce in themselves a physiological state of quietude (including a drop in heart rate, metabolic rate, and breathing rate). And this state of quietude has remarkably favorable benefit for people's health. He first postulated that there were 4 essential components for the relaxation response: a quiet environment, a mental device to occupy the mind, a passive attitude, and a comfortable position. But further investigation revealed that a quiet place and a comfortable position were unnecessary; the only essential factors for the relaxation response were a mental device to occupy the mind and a passive attitude—and of the two, a passive attitude was the more crucial. This passive attitude is alternatively described as "putting aside destructive thoughts," "an emptying of all thoughts and distractions from one's mind,""being freed from petty cares," "a cessation of the intellect and desires," "adopting a let-it-happen attitude."

The approaches therapists use to promote relaxation include deep breathing, progressive muscle relaxation, and meditation (being in the present). [4] The client is taught these skills and then asked to practice them for several weeks until they become more the client's usual way of being. Of help is the fact that each of these skills promotes the others—deep breathing relaxes the body, relaxing the body promotes deep breathing, and they both interact in a similar manner with being in the present. The key component is being in the present rather than in one's head; deep breathing and keeping one's body loose and relaxed are important mainly insofar as they foster that. Conversely, getting pulled out of the present and more into one's head produces constricted breathing and physical tenseness.

Deep breathing means breathing with your abdomen rather than just shallow upper chest breathing. When you practice, place a hand on your abdomen beneath your rib cage; that hand should rise and fall as you inhale and exhale. Take long slow deep breaths, counting to 4 while you inhale and again as you exhale. If you have trouble learning this kind of breathing, try extending your hands over your head while lying down or clasping your hands behind your back while sitting (both open up the chest for easier deep breathing). Deep diaphragmatic breathing promotes muscle relaxation and a quiet mind. This is a skill easily learned and helpful for a state of relaxation.

Progressive muscle relaxation is a process where you systematically go through the main muscle groups of the body—first tensing the muscle and then releasing it. The muscle groups include the fists, biceps, triceps, forehead, muscles around the eyes, jaws, back of the neck, shoulders, shoulder blades, chest, stomach, lower back, buttocks, thighs, calves, and toes. This method of relaxation is effective, although requiring more time to learn than deep breathing; indeed anxiety cannot exist in a relaxed body.

The primary aim of meditation is to produce a nonjudgmental, passive attitude—to calm the mind. Meditation attempts to teach the person to just be, to let go of thoughts and simply focus on being in the here and now. When thoughts come, the person is instructed neither to hold on to them nor to reject them too vigorously, but just to allow them to come and go. People with great difficulty quieting their mind at first may need to employ some "mental device to occupy the mind" as suggested by Benson; a preoccupied mind is less susceptible to out of control thinking. Examples include using a mantra (thought or spoken with each breath) like "Om" or "Let go, let God," counting each breath, imaging a peaceful scene, or feeling a warm liquid or light spreading through one's body. The meditation approach to relaxation is more difficult than deep breathing or progressive muscle relaxation because, to be truly effective, it requires a profound change in one's attitude about life.

Clients relate more readily to the concept of being in the present than they do to meditation (even though essentially they are the same). True meditation is a deeply ingrained state of being, a way of living rather than something practiced for a certain period of time—and that way of living is to be intensely in the present. Focus your attention more and more on the present, the here and now. If that reality is pleasant, enjoy and appreciate your good fortune. If it is unpleasant, try to find it interesting rather than depressing or irritating. Methods that help clients in my practice to be more in the present include using a physical anchor like pinching themselves, rubbing their face or hands, or feeling themselves breathing or their weight in the chair; observing their environment so they could describe it later; or experiencing themselves in the process of being. Richard Carlson, Ph. D. suggests another method:

> An interesting exercise is to block out periods of time where you commit to doing only one thing at a time. Whether you're washing dishes, talking on the phone, driving a car, playing with your child, talking to your spouse, or reading a magazine, try to focus only on that one thing. Be present in what you are doing. Concentrate. You'll notice two things beginning to happen. First, you'll actually enjoy what you are doing, even something mundane, like washing dishes or cleaning out a closet. When you're focused, rather than distracted, it enables you to become absorbed and interested in your activity, whatever it might be. Second, you'll be amazed at how quickly and efficiently you'll get things done. [5]

After explaining these relaxation methods and giving clients a chance to practice them, I ask clients to monitor themselves 5 or 6 times a day: to notice their breathing and change it if warranted, to notice their body and make it more relaxed if necessary, to notice whether or not they are in the present and promote that change if not. Ironically, being aware that you aren't in the present puts you back in the present, even if only for a few seconds.

Doing this self-monitoring for a month or so leads many clients to a greater degree of relaxation as their general state. But the relaxation techniques are relatively ineffective with neurotic individuals. There are few magical cures in life and the relaxation techniques are not a magical cure for the misery experienced in neurosis. Sometimes you can't get there from here. Because of their deeply ingrained resistance to life, there are no peaceful, happy, relaxed neurotics.

Being less in one's head is crucial for being at peace with life; but being at peace with life requires a second component—the unconditional acceptance of reality as it is. Together these two factors lead to a profound sense of peace and tranquility, a profound sense of happiness. Albert Ellis, one of the most influential psychologists of our time and founder of Rational Emotive Behavior Therapy, points out that psychological health can only be attained through unconditional acceptance of oneself, other people, and life in general.[6] Without such unconditional acceptance, the relaxation techniques may help a person feel better but they won't produce lasting change and happiness.

Dan Millman provides insight into this unconditional acceptance of reality:

If you don't get what you want, you suffer; if you get what you don't want, you suffer; even when you get exactly what you want, you still suffer because you can't hold onto it forever. Your mind is your predicament. It wants to be free of change, free of pain, free of the obligations of life and death. But change is a law, and no amount of pretending will alter that reality.... Life is not suffering; it's just that you will suffer it, rather than enjoy it, until you let go of your mind's attachments and just go for the ride freely, no matter what happens. [7]

This approach to life involves unconditional acceptance of life as it is. People struggle with life because they want and even insist it be a certain way, rather than as Millman suggests, "go for the ride freely, no matter what happens." This is what Eastern thought means by "going with the flow." There is commitment to present moment reality, however it presents itself. As the saying goes, "If life gives you lemons, make lemonade." The secret to happiness is to not need reality to be any particular way. True security lies not in the things one has but in the things one can do without. Profound tranquility and happiness result from being attentive to and unconditionally accepting of present moment reality. Give your full attention to the present, whether or not it conforms to what you like. This is meditation and the surest road to peace and happiness. You cannot attain happiness; when you accept reality as it is, when you surrender all the conditions you think you need to be happy, happiness attains you.

The following eighteenth-century Sufi story points out the wisdom of this unconditional acceptance of life. Anything that happens can be survived and maybe even turned into our best interest.

Once in a city in the Farthest West there lived a girl called Fatima. She was the daughter of a prosperous spinner. One day her father said to her: "Come, daughter; we are going on a journey, for I have business in the islands of the Middle Sea. Perhaps you may find some handsome youth in a good situation whom you could take as husband."

They set off and traveled from island to island, the father doing his trading while Fatima dreamt of the husband who might soon be hers. One day, however, they were on the way to Crete when a storm blew up, and the ship was wrecked. Fatima, only half-conscious, was cast up on the seashore near Alexandria. Her father was dead, and she was utterly destitute.

She could only remember dimly her life until then, for her experience of the shipwreck, and her exposure in the sea, had utterly exhausted her.

While she was wandering on the sands, a family of cloth-makers found her. Although they were poor, they took her into their humble home and taught her their craft. Thus it was that she made a second life for herself, and within a year or two she was happy and reconciled to her lot. But one day, when she was on the seashore for some reason, a band of slave-traders landed and carried her, along with other captives, away with them.

Although she bitterly lamented her lot, Fatima found no sympathy from the slavers, who took her to Istanbul and sold her as a slave.

Her world had collapsed for the second time. Now it chanced that there were few buyers at the market. One of them was a man who was looking for slaves to work in his woodyard, where he made masts for ships. When he saw the dejection of the unfortunate Fatima, he decided to buy her, thinking that in this way, at least, he might be able to give her a slightly better life than if she were bought by someone else.

He took Fatima to his home, intending to make her a serving-maid for his wife. When he arrived at the house, however, he found that he had lost all his money in a cargo which had been captured by pirates. He could not afford workers, so he, Fatima and his wife were left alone to work at the heavy labour of making masts.

Fatima, grateful to her employer for rescuing her, worked so hard and so well that he gave her her freedom, and she became his trusted helper. Thus it was that she became comparatively happy in her third career.

One day he said to her: "Fatima, I want you to go with a cargo of ships' masts to Java, as my agent, and be sure that you sell them at a profit."

She set off, but when the ship was off the coast of China a typhoon wrecked it, and Fatima found herself again cast up on the seashore of a strange land. Once again she wept bitterly, for she felt that nothing in her life was working in accordance with expectation. Whenever things seemed to be going well, something came and destroyed all her hopes.

"Why is it," she cried out, for the third time, "that whenever I try to do something it comes to grief? Why should so many unfortunate things happen to me?" But there was no answer. So she picked herself up from the sand, and started to walk inland.

Now it so happened that nobody in China had heard of Fatima, or knew anything about her troubles. But there was a legend that a certain stranger, a woman, would one day arrive there, and that she would be able to make a tent for the Emperor. And, since there was as yet nobody in China who could make tents, everyone looked upon the fulfillment of this prediction with the liveliest anticipation.

In order to make sure that this stranger, when she arrived, would not be missed, successive Emperors of China had followed the custom of sending heralds, once a year, to all the towns and villages of the land, asking for any foreign woman to be produced at Court.

When Fatima stumbled into a town by the Chinese seashore, it was one such occasion. The people spoke to her through an interpreter, and explained that she would have to go to see the Emperor.

"Lady," said the Emperor, when Fatima was brought before him, "can you make a tent?"

"I think so," said Fatima.

She asked for rope, but there was none to be had. So, remembering her time as a spinner, she collected flax and made ropes. Then she asked for stout cloth, but the Chinese had none of the kind which she needed. So, drawing on her experience with the weavers of Alexandria,

24

she made some stout tent cloth. Then she found that she needed tent-poles, but there were none in China. So Fatima, remembering how she had been trained by the wood-fashioner of Istanbul, cunningly made stout tent poles. When these were ready, she racked her brains for the memory of all the tents she had seen in her travels; and lo, a tent was made.

When this wonder was revealed to the Emperor of China, he offered Fatima the fulfillment of any wish she cared to name. She chose to settle in China, where she married a handsome prince, and where she remained in happiness, surrounded by her children, until the end of her days.

It was through these adventures that Fatima realized that what had appeared to be an unpleasant experience at the time, turned out to be an essential part of the making of her ultimate happiness. [8]

Richard Bandler and John Grinder point out that the wise man's happiness and tranquility does not depend on the temporarily fortunate or unfortunate things that happen in life:

A very old Chinese Taoist story describes a farmer in a poor country village. He was considered very well to do, because he owned a horse which he used for plowing and for transportation. One day his horse ran away. All his neighbors exclaimed how terrible this was, but the farmer simply said "Maybe."

A few days later the horse returned and brought two wild horses with it. The neighbors *all rejoiced at his good fortune, but the farmer just said "Maybe."*

The next day the farmer's son tried to ride one of the wild horses; the horse threw him and broke his leg. The neighbors all offered their sympathy for his misfortune, but the farmer again said "Maybe."

The next week conscription officers came to the village to take young men for the army. They rejected the farmer's son because of his broken leg. When the neighbors told him how lucky he was, the farmer replied "Maybe...." [9]

Many people spend life afraid their horse will run away (or depressed because it did run away) rather than deal with life on whatever terms it presents itself. Be accepting of life as it occurs—not passively, but by making the best of it. More important than what happens to you, is to live life, to deal with life events as meaningfully as possible, and then to be unreasonably happy. Anyone can be happy when he gets what he wants; it takes a truly healthy person to be happy regardless, without any reason whatsoever. That is what true mental health is all about.

Each day that I go to work, and each day that I don't go to work, I remind myself of the importance of enjoying that day. I want to feel myself breathe, see and hear other people and the world around me. Regardless of what happens, I owe it to myself to enjoy the process of living—one day at a time, moment-by-moment, always in the present. Living too often gets sacrificed in order to get things done; we need to place more emphasis on the process of life as opposed to accomplishments and productivity. Life is not about getting a grade; it's about living. And paradoxically, the more one is in the present, rather than rigidly focused on getting things done, the more effective he will be and the more he will accomplish.

One of my favorite sayings is "If something is worth doing, it's worth doing poorly." I enjoy golf a great deal—not because I've mastered the game but because I can golf with mediocrity either right- or left-handed. I try to enjoy, and learn from both my common mistakes and my occasional moments of athletic brilliance. I find it interesting that I am vulnerable to the same basic mistakes regardless of which side I play from; but at least I can choose whether to be victimized right- or left-handed. But more importantly, I can choose to be on the golf course experiencing the wonderful gift of today—regardless of how I score, who I play with, what today's weather is like, whether the course of play is slow or wide-open. In contrast, the more I get into hating my ineptitude at the game, the worse I invariably play.

My main hobby is ultra marathons—commonly runs of 50 miles or more on dirt trails through parks and forests. This hobby produces an absence of self-talk; not paying attention to the trail invariably produces a nasty fall. There are activities like this that are naturally meditative; fishing is like that for many people—a relatively mindless repetitive behavior in some beautiful setting. Such activities have Herbert Benson's "mental device to occupy the mind" built in. But the key is to live all of life in such a meditative way—a way intensively focused on the present. Richard Carlson, Ph. D. comments: "As you focus more on becoming more peaceful with where you are, rather than focusing on where you would rather be, you begin to find peace right now, in the present. Then, as you move around, try new things, and meet new people, you carry that sense of inner peace with you."[10]

We're all too busy trying to get somewhere, trying to make life what we think it needs to be, instead of truly being where we are. Trying to get somewhere is fine as long as we realize that we don't need to get there to be happy, as long as we remember to enjoy the process of trying to get there. All we ever have is the present. If we aren't in the present today, we likely won't be in the present tomorrow. If we aren't happy now, we are at great risk for never being happy.

Western civilization over-values thinking. French philosopher Descartes' statement, "I think, therefore I am" could just as sensibly have been stated: "I see, therefore I am;" "I hear, therefore I am;" "I feel myself breathe, therefore I am." In my seminary philosophy classes, we were presented with logic that supposedly proved the existence of God; we ingeniously used the same logic to prove the existence of Santa Claus. Psychotherapy has become almost exclusively oriented toward helping clients correct their thinking (Cognitive Therapy); but this approach ignores the reality that people think too much, that they rely on thinking for a degree of certitude that is unrealistic and neurotic. Just as you can't prove or disprove the existence of yourself, God, or Santa Claus, you can't prove your own value or worth. There are things you simply have to believe or not believe; they are matters of faith, philosophy, or experience—not logic. Thinking too much, being too much in one's head, is as destructive as distorted thinking.

There are positive uses of the mind—analyzing, concentrating, being attentive, recalling, planning, creating. Be leery, however, of your mind's endeavors that don't involve some specific useful function. The undisciplined mind can be out of control and destructive: obsessing, worrying, judging oneself unnecessarily harshly and negatively, being distracted. These are activities of the mind that serve no useful function and only destroy tranquility and negatively impact one's ability to function. Such activities of the mind result from neurotic resistance to life, an exaggerated need for control, the inability to accept life as it is. This is the mind malfunctioning. Unless your conscious mind is performing a specific useful function, keep it free and clear—allowing yourself to experience fully the present moment. Out of such neurotic factors, we also trust our conscious mind more than our subconscious mind, our analytic left brain more than our creative right-brain.

Being in the present rather than in one's head, and accepting reality as it is, leads to more effective functioning; there's less distraction and your subconscious mind can be more creative. Benson's years of research showed that profound relaxation promotes better concentration and other mental functions as well as increased spontaneity and creativity. In addition, this approach to life is likely to produce results more in accord with your desires. I frequently see clients who are desperately trying to get their spouse or significant other to return to them. This will go on for months with the person losing all this time out of depression and their unwillingness to commit to reality however it presents itself. The more desperate and depressed they are, the greater their need for love, the less the other person is likely to be attracted to them; their partner will despise and be turned off by their neediness and weakness. Many things in life function according to some perverted "catch 22" laws of reality. If you want or need something desperately, it will elude your grasp (to help you realize that you truly don't need it). The minute you realize you don't need it, it will fall in your lap. The need to control life often produces precisely what the person is trying to prevent.

This unconditional acceptance of life isn't devoid of emotion, just neurotic emotion. I'm not advocating the stoicism reflected in the story of the Buddha who, upon being informed that his son had just died in a tragic accident, responded, "Well I always knew he wasn't immortal." But consider the person who has been depressed since his/her parents died 5 or 6 years ago in their eighties. This is neurotic resistance to life, not healthy grief. Healthy people experience painful grief and sorrow, but it doesn't linger and fester into something manufactured (neurotic emotionality). And in the absence of neurotic emotionality, genuine emotions can be more fully experienced.

This unconditional acceptance of reality isn't fatalistic. Fatalistic resignation, as a matter of fact, is just a passive form of resisting life by refusing to engage life fully. The healthy person makes every attempt to make life what he wants; but he then completely accepts what happens. He lives with purpose and determination, but in a non-resistive manner. He doesn't fear what might happen; he doesn't experience anger, depression, self-pity, or guilt over what does happen—even when that is not what he wanted or attempted to make happen. An uncompromising commitment to the present, to living, leads to less fear and anxiety, less depression, less anger. It leads to more happiness, more humor, more ability to love. True happiness comes when one surrenders to and fully experiences reality rather than resisting or attempting to control reality.

The journey to psychological health is a life long struggle; but, as the reader will learn, difficulty and adversity can be enjoyed rather than merely endured. As mentioned, there are no peaceful neurotics. The path to psychological health involves learning to avoid various neurotic roadblocks. As will be clarified, we all have neurotic tendencies but we don't have to be neurotic—and the difference between the two is profound. This is a book of great hope; it attempts to uncover the hidden obstacles along life's journey so that life can be lived with prevailing tranquility and happiness. Being firmly anchored in the present (thinking less but being more aware), combined with unconditional acceptance of reality as it is, makes life a truly rewarding experience.

1 — *Constructive Living*, by David Reynolds (Honolulu: University of Hawaii Press, 1984), p. 60.

2 — *Your Erroneous Zones*, by Wayne W. Dyer (New York: Avon Books, 1977), p. 232. Reprinted by permission of HarperCollins Publishers Inc.

3 — *The Relaxation Response*, by Herbert Benson (New York: Morrow, 1975).

4 — *The Anxiety and Phobia Workbook*, Third Edition, by Edmund Bourne (Oakland: New Harbinger Publications, 2001) serves as an excellent resource in this regard.

5 — *Don't Sweat the Small Stuff...and It's All Small Stuff*, by Richard Carlson (New York: Hyperion, 1997), p. 152. Reprinted by permission of Hyperion.

6 — *Feeling Better, Getting Better, Staying Better*, by Albert Ellis (Atascadero, California: Impact Publishers, 2001).

7 — *The Way of the Peaceful Warrior*, by Dan Millman, p. 61. Used with permission from New World Library, Novato, CA, 94949, www.newworldlibrary.com

8 — *Tales of the Dervishes*, by Idries Shaw (London: Octagon Press, 1982), pp. 72-74.

9 — *Reframing*, by Richard Bandler and John Grinder (Moab, Utah: Real People Press, 1982), p. 1.

10 — *Don't Sweat the Small Stuff...and It's All Small Stuff*, by Richard Carlson (New York: Hyperion, 1997), p. 134. Reprinted by permission of Hyperion.

Chapter TWO
HOW TO HAVE HEALTHY SELF-ESTEEM

You may choose to climb the highest available mountain
for several good reasons. You may enjoy climbing; may
delight in the challenge this difficult peak presents; or
may thrill to the view from the top. But you also may
have bad reasons for climbing the same mountain: to
look down and spit on the people below.
Albert Ellis Ph. D. and Robert Harper Ph. D. [11]

The first major obstacle in the struggle for
psychological health—the ability to live fully
and be oneself—involves problems pertaining
to self-esteem. On the one hand people crave rank
and status, prestige, being better than others (the
neurotic search for glory). On the other hand they
doubt their value and importance, fearing that in reality
they are worthless and insignificant (the neurotic
obsession with inferiority).

Milton Erickson, M. D. a renowned deceased
therapist, displayed a card in his office that on the
outside read, "When you think of all the stars in our
galaxy and all the galaxies in the universe, doesn't it
make you feel humble and insignificant?" The inside
read, "Me neither." Unfortunately most of us don't
resolve this issue that readily or that favorably. Instead
we struggle with life—feeling insignificant, un-
important, and inferior to others. We judge ourselves
and hold ourselves accountable for measuring up to
certain standards. Regardless of the standards we use,

often our self-evaluation is not very positive. Being human means that we have flaws we wish we didn't have, that we have done things we are ashamed of and wish we hadn't done. In the course of life we make mistakes, we perform below what we might have done given our best effort. But even when we do our best, we often fail, do poorly, or realize that others might have done better. This is unavoidably part of the human condition.

All therapists see a great number of clients with terrible self-esteem, most presenting with depression. It's difficult to live when you have poor self-esteem; you have little confidence in yourself and your ability to deal effectively with life. It's not surprising that many people with poor self-esteem suffer depression. In turn low self-esteem commonly becomes more severe as part of the process of being depressed. Depressed people see themselves as failures in a world where everyone else is doing great; they forget that "to err is human." They see themselves as ugly, stupid, immoral—distasteful and inferior in every way imaginable. The worse they feel about themselves the more depressed they become; the more depressed they become the worse they feel about themselves.

Unfortunately low self-esteem is not limited to these millions of Americans suffering clinical depression; it pervades the life of millions more who struggle on without zest, enthusiasm, or hopeful anticipation. Most of us have a difficult time not feeling inferior—let alone feeling good about ourselves. It's easy to understand how people lose good self-esteem; it seems deeply rooted in the human condition. Life seems more to beat people down—with its common abuse and mistreatment, failure and disappointment, loss and tragedy—than to help them feel good about themselves. Children who are the victim of sexual abuse feel it is because there is something wrong with them; somehow it is their fault. Getting downsized takes a toll on the victim's self-esteem, even when it is clear it had nothing to do with him or the quality of his work. When bad things happen in life, which is inevitable, there is a tendency to feel inferior, inadequate, guilty. Unfortunately the corresponding tendency to feel better self-esteem when good things happen does not appear as innate, powerful, or pervasive.

Being out of balance on the issue of self-esteem in the opposite direction can be equally unhealthy and destructive. Low self-esteem is more prevalent than grandiosity; but inflated self-esteem makes living as difficult or impossible as self-depreciation—just in a different way. Arrogance, being self-centered, being taken up with oneself alienates others; nobody likes the person who talks too much about himself, who boasts, who monopolizes the conversation—whether in the work environment, social setting, or intimate relationships. Such people often fail to get what they want in the various areas of life because they irritate others. But more importantly, and less well understood, inflated self-esteem creates pressure to measure up to standards which interferes with one's ability to be tranquil and in the present. Grandiosity creates insecurity and fear of failure; it's difficult to enjoy life when you need so badly to impress and excel.

Therapists see far fewer grandiose clients than clients with low self-esteem—after all if you're great why would you need therapy? Narcissism is grandiosity at its worst; narcissists are so self-aggrandizing and so infatuated with themselves that they discount others as insignificant in comparison. Occasionally narcissists get seen in therapy because their narcissism gets so out of control as to involve psychotic delusions of greatness—ideas they are Jesus Christ or God's specially chosen agent, or so powerful they could save or destroy the universe. I recently saw a 51-year-old man who had 5 hospitalizations many years ago with psychotic grandiose delusions. For years he did fine on psychiatric medications; but when I saw him, he was not doing fine. He was again having grandiose thoughts: the world would end if he didn't perform a certain ritual, his wife would die if he didn't say a certain prayer. A friend had loaned him the tapes "Conversations with God;" he so desperately needed to be incredibly important and powerful that he expanded that message into blatant distortion of reality.

The solution to these problems regarding self-esteem is not clear. Theoretically religion provides a foundation for healthy self-esteem—with its dual tenets that (1) we are created in God's image, and yet (2) every person requires repentance and salvation. Unfortunately people with low self-esteem often react to religion in ways that more promote guilt and shame than better self-esteem; people with inflated self-esteem often use religion (like the man discussed above) as a forum for their grandiosity and thus make their grandiosity even more extreme. As mentioned, people with inflated self-esteem seldom seek psychotherapy; when they do, therapy often is of little benefit. People with low self-esteem frequently seek psychotherapy, but therapists struggle endlessly and futilely in their efforts to improve these clients' self-esteem.

Cognitive Therapists[12] commonly attempt to solve the problem of low self-esteem by correcting the client's faulty thinking (cognitive distortions). Among the errors and inconsistencies in our process of judging ourselves, they point out that:

- The standards we use to judge ourselves are unrealistic and arbitrary.

- To err is human—yet we measure ourselves against a standard of perfection.

- We judge ourselves more harshly than we judge our family members, friends, or even strangers.

- The fact that I failed at a given task needs to be tempered with such realizations as the fact that it wasn't a total failure, that I did fine on some other task, or that I may not be a success in the work world but I am a wonderful husband or father.

Regardless of how cleverly the therapist points out their cognitive distortions, however, these clients tend to return over and over to their areas of inadequacy and failure. They are so fixated on their inferiority, lack of value, or shame the therapist would have to prove their value, worth, and goodness—and unfortunately this is not something that can be proven. As a result, these Cognitive Therapists ultimately resort back to the position of unconditional self-acceptance first put forth in the psychological literature by Albert Ellis[13] in the 1970's—an individual's worth, or lack of worth, can't be proven; the best approach is to assume that we have worth and value simply because we exist. There's no need to evaluate or rate ourselves; and doing that, in reality, causes many of our more serious emotional problems.

As this chapter will clarify, trying to prove your worth is ultimately doomed to failure because self-worth cannot be proven. Not only is the attempt to achieve good self-esteem through correcting your cognitive distortions a futile venture; it lends itself to neurosis. Not only does it foster being self-preoccupied, it keeps you locked in your mind (devising counter arguments) rather than living in the present as advocated in the previous chapter. When you quit judging yourself altogether, you are more available for living with intensity and concentration. Doing so allows you to think less and to live more; it allows you to accept both life and yourself as they are. In the process of living fully, you realize your value and worth.

I offer two solutions for developing healthy self-esteem. The first is arrived at in response to the problem of low self-esteem, the second in response to the problem of inflated self-esteem. Not as surprising as it might seem at first glance, the two solutions have much in common. Psychological theory has long argued that narcissists really have low self-esteem; otherwise, why do they so desperately need to feel superior? One could argue likewise that people with low self-esteem are too preoccupied with themselves and their own worth. Both low self-esteem and inflated self-esteem are manifestations of egocentricity—the neurotic excessive concern with self.

The solution to the problem of low self-esteem involves the realization that it's a trap to believe you need good self-esteem to live life. Good self-esteem is based on meeting certain standards or criteria, and conditional worth is fragile and insecure. You cannot earn self-worth through your accomplishments and you don't lose self-worth through your failures. Self-worth based on accomplishments is fragile and ultimately doomed to failure; the loss of self-worth based on lack of accomplishments is the core of neurotic depression. Healthy people don't gloat over their successes and they don't get depressed over their failures. There are happy physicians and happy maintenance workers, just as there are unhappy physicians and unhappy maintenance workers.

Every criterion ever devised for measuring self-worth is dependent on cultural values; and different cultures and subcultures base a person's worth on something different: attractiveness, intelligence, popularity, devotion to God, accomplishments, altruism, character, a strong work ethic, loyalty to cultural values and tradition. None of these criteria can make you a more worthwhile person or better than anyone else. No matter which of these subjective criteria you use to measure your worth, there will be times when you don't measure up very favorably; that doesn't make you a less valuable person than you were before. You are still the same person, with the same worth and value, carrying on in life as best you can given your resources—including your flaws and weaknesses. You do the best you can; welcome to the human family. True self-esteem is the ability to like and respect yourself as much when you fail as when you succeed; it is unconditional. Richard Carlson, Ph. D. comments:

> I once heard of a proposed book title that sums up the message of this strategy: *I'm not Okay, You're not Okay, and that's Okay.* Give yourself a break. No one is going to bat 100 percent, or even close to it. All that's important is that, generally speaking, you are doing your best and that you are moving in the right direction.[14]

Being alive is reason enough to ensure our worth and validity; every living person has a right to breathe and take up space on the planet. We don't have to earn or prove anything. Our worth is not dependent on meeting certain criteria or being better than others; it is our unconditional birthright. Life and our right to live is an unearned gift. The sun comes up each day for everyone alike; the fish bite just as well for the lowly as for the mighty. Any healthy parent loves each of their children unconditionally; the child doesn't have to meet any certain standard or prove anything. Doesn't it make sense that we owe ourselves the same unconditional acceptance? Yet people show greater compassion for others than for themselves; they judge themselves more harshly than others. People call themselves "stupid," "worthless" or "inept"—all in ways they would never talk to their best friend. We don't look down on or despise others because they failed at something or made a poor decision. We don't berate or ridicule others because they showed poor judgment or didn't work as hard at something as they might have. We don't demand that others prove their worth or right to be alive. If you haven't already done so, it's time to claim your birthright. You owe yourself compassion, forgiveness, unconditional love and acceptance; your worth and your right to live don't have to be earned or proven.

I personally believe some people destroy their innate worth and validity, their right to live life as an unearned gift—people such as Adolf Hitler, savage mass-murderers or chronic child molesters (whether they became evil through their own volition or whether early life events and experiences were so horrendous as to make such a result inevitable). Such people, if they had a conscience, justifiably would feel boundless shame and guilt. Fortunately such people are rare; unfortunately the incidence of people who unjustly treat and think of themselves as if they were so horrendous is common. Worth or self-esteem is not something that has to be earned, but it is something that can be destroyed by living so destructively that the human spirit is destroyed beyond repair.

The solution to the problem of inflated self-esteem involves balancing grandiosity with humility; as well as becoming less self-preoccupied and less self-centered. The problem in the instance of the man referred to above with the thoughts that only he could save the world or save his wife was a lack of balance; grandiosity needs desperately to be balanced with humility. As John F Kennedy pointed out, "Extraordinary things are done by ordinary people." Healthy people believe in themselves, but they also believe in and support other people in their process of fulfilling their potential. They strive more to be great than to be better than others. They are not conceited but humble. Their strength grows out of their acceptance of weakness and humanity. Gestalt Therapy has a saying that "You can only be strong when you can accept being weak." In a similar vein, you can only have healthy self-esteem, and only meaningfully strive for greatness, when you acknowledge and accept your flaws and failures but realize they don't matter.

I am writing this during the "Tiger Woods phenomenon." It's fascinating the way he has been accepted, how the TV ratings soar the more insurmountable his lead grows. Often a winner is resented more than supported and a "multi-cultural" man dominating what traditionally has been a "white man's game" could have leant itself to that (consider all the people who threatened Henry Aaron's life when he approached Babe Ruth's home run record). I don't know Tiger Woods personally, but the Tiger Woods we all know through the media (whether it matches reality or is just a created image) is hard not to like. Here is someone who decided at an early age to become the greatest golfer in the world, maybe in history; that's pretty grandiose. But now that he has accomplished that goal, he doesn't boast or gloat—he's humble (and grandiosity balanced with humility is healthy and inspirational). He doesn't put himself above others. He talks about needing to work on some aspect of his game, he talks about the good luck he had on a certain hole. One of the unusual aspects of this phenomenon is his gaining this humility early in life.

We are not the center of the universe; we are not God. We are not better or more valuable than any other human being. I once saw a woman in therapy who went to prison for fraud to have money to feed and provide for her children (her husband used their money for alcohol). I'm sure she made poor choices and decisions all along the course that led to the theft, but maybe she showed more love and courage than you or I could ever manage. There but for the grace of God go I.

In my professional practice, when clients call me doctor I inform them that I prefer they call me by my first name—adding the joke that when people call me doctor, they expect too much. I know a lot about psychology and how to help people change, but that doesn't make me better than them. My auto mechanic hopefully knows a lot about cars and how to keep my car running but I don't refer to him as "sir" or "honorable mechanic." In psychotherapy the client is encouraged to drop pretenses and deal openly with personal life issues; it seems more consistent with that expectation for me to unpretentiously go by my first name. If I allow or even foster or insist on being called doctor, that sets a tone suggesting that I am superior or should be held in higher esteem than my client. But I remain the same person who shoveled manure out of pens as a child on the farm; having a doctoral degree in psychology notwithstanding, I am no better than my client or anyone else.

Both narcissists and people with low self-esteem are too preoccupied with themselves—one desperately needing to be superior to others, the other desperately trying to not feel inferior to others. Both miss the point entirely. The important reality is life and the chance to be part of it. As Dan Millman points out, the best self-concept is none at all.

The undesirability of a low self-concept may seem obvious, since it limits our achievement. Yet, an unrealistically high self-concept has its own unique problems. A young child who is praised for everything gets used to being praised. Praise represents positive energy and attention which all children crave. He will strive to maintain this praise as much as possible. He may even develop precocious abilities. This child's sense of self-worth will depend upon achievement and success. He expects himself to succeed—and projects this onto the world, so that it seems everyone else expects him to succeed too. There can be tremendous psychic pressure not to let the world down. This pressure can create brilliant students, star athletes...and suicides.

Unrealistically high or low self-concept is debilitating. The best self-concept is none at all. A child raised in a home relatively free from exaggerations of praise or blame will just take a realistic, experimental, and persevering approach to his pursuits, without undue psychic pressure. He achieves naturally, in good time, with ordinary enjoyment.[15]

The most miserable people are those who are self-focused, who feel the constant need to prove their worth. The most peaceful people have given away their sense of self; such people live and grow old gracefully—they are able to live fully and intensely because they are not distracted by a need to prove anything. They have less ego involvement. They know the world could and eventually will do fine without them. They talk not so much about what they have accomplished, which takes no courage at all, but about the things in life that fascinate them and about what they plan or hope to accomplish in the future. They are not afraid to set high goals because they are not afraid to fail. They think more about life and living and less about themselves and proving their worth. Ironically the way to develop a better sense of self is to be less self-oriented and more focused on life and humanity. This not only circumvents the problems connected to self-evaluation; it leads to being a psychologically healthier, more mature person. Self-concept is simply one aspect of being self-preoccupied and self-centered; it is a breeding ground for all neurotic emotions and behavior. Healthy people are neither self-preoccupied nor self-centered; they are more interested in life and living than worried about their own worth.

An extension of being less self-preoccupied is to be less oriented toward what is mine: my children, my spouse, my family, my city, my country, my ethnic group, my religion. Healthy people care about these things, but they also care about all humanity. They are more oriented toward the family of man than just their own biological family.

Greatness occurs most naturally in someone not desperately needing to be better than others, in someone not needing to prove his basic worth. In the process of maturing, the healthy person becomes less egocentric and experiences ever-increasing joy and satisfaction in being a valuable, unique part of the family of man—rather than looking down on and despising others in comparison. In contrast, "the neurotic is at bottom unrelated to the group. He does not feel part of it, does not have a feeling of belonging, but rather uses it for his personal prestige."[16]

Live with dedication and purpose. Pursue whatever seems important or worthwhile to you—self-growth, making the world a better place, helping others, enjoying life more. Take classes, read, improve your social skills, lose weight, join a fitness center, promote into management, learn a new skill. But do these things because they are enjoyable or worthwhile—rather than as an attempt to feel okay about yourself or somehow better than others. Living free of egocentric needs and concerns provides a healthier philosophical basis for living that can lead to a psychologically healthier life.

Let's use chess as an example. While I don't play chess, it seems like a wonderful activity because, while one can always improve, the game can never be mastered. One can play chess at many different levels, from a casual fun pastime or hobby to a serious life passion. Playing at any level is fine, whatever pleases you. But if your goal is to become a great chess player, to excel, don't fall into the trap of using the game to prove your greatness, to prove yourself better than others. It's fine to use the game to challenge yourself and your will and determination. There's nothing wrong with striving to become the best player at whatever level you choose. But remember to love the game, to appreciate your opponents and comrades who also love chess. Think how frustrating it would be to be a great chess player and suddenly not have anyone else be interested in the game—no one to play, no one to talk to about the game, no one to teach and learn from. Remember to learn from your mistakes rather than be devastated by them. Marvel at an opponent's brilliance rather than be a poor loser. Ironically if your goal is to become the best player, the need to prove your worth will only get in your way of accomplishing that goal. Once a person wins for the first time, he is more likely to win again because he is less likely to have as great a need to prove himself and as a result to be less afraid of failure and better able to use his skill and ability.

We all need a sense of importance, a niche, our place in the sun. Striving, ambition, desire is a valuable aspect of being human; but it needs to be kept in balance and perspective. People with inflated self-esteem are compulsively driven by their need for glory and recognition, striving to become what others admire rather than asserting who they truly are. As we lose the neurotic obsession with glory, we become free to live and be ourselves. We become more interested in growing and living than excelling over others.

Less often recognized as unhealthy, compared to the neurotic search for glory, is the neurotic negation of self. Psychological health requires a commitment to being oneself and fulfilling one's potential. Many people lack the courage to truly live. Out of fear they never enter the arena of life, never assert themselves and the importance of their life. In all its various forms (codependency, martyrdom, perfectionism, withdrawal, lack of drive and ambition) such people restrict and curtail themselves. They justify their resignation, lack of drive and effort, their refusal to become engaged with life under the guise of saintliness and unselfishness. Rather than struggling to make life what they want, and then accepting whatever happens, they want and expect nothing. They commit the worst form of disrespect for life—refusing to recognize and assert the importance of life and being who they were meant to be.

While it can be difficult to differentiate between healthy surrender of self and unhealthy negation of self (because the behavior is often similar), the subjective experience and the quality of the behavior is very different. Mother Teresa was fulfilled by her service of others. She didn't whine, complain, or express regret; she wasn't depressed, miserable, or resentful. She actualized herself through her behavior rather than being restricted or limited by it, and she experienced great peace and happiness in the process.

Be who you are instead of comparing yourself to others, instead of judging yourself. This leaves you free to live. I encourage clients not to strive to be "normal." It's your life—you owe it to yourself to pursue your goals and dreams, your hopes and ambitions; to be who you are and who you want to become. Never compromise your rarity and uniqueness just to fit in, to be accepted by others, to be what others want. Your life is too valuable to squander in the pursuit of appearing to be like everyone else, to be concerned about what others think of you. Go out of your way to let others know what you believe and feel. Form your own ideas, your own preferences, your own personality, your own sense of humor. You were born a unique individual; develop that uniqueness. Keep alive your hope of doing great things with your life; never settle for a life of mediocrity. Make it your goal to be a great person rather than to be better than others. Support others in their efforts to do likewise. As Og Mandino comments, "God will do nothing without man and whenever He works a miracle it is always done through man."[17]

Not everyone is capable of playing golf like Tiger Woods or being president of the United States; but we don't need to be. We can all love, help others, care; and who among us would view that as trivial? And often we are capable of more than we give ourselves credit for. Dare to be great. Don't try to be like others; proclaim your rarity. Be who you are, a person with unique and valuable qualities. Live your life to the fullest, with the firm conviction that to do otherwise would be an injustice to the world. But remember always to be humble—grandiosity balanced with humility is healthy. You don't have to prove yourself or your worth—that is your birthright. Healthy self-esteem is neither poor self-esteem nor good self-esteem; it is based on the realization that everyone is unique and valuable, yourself included. What is important isn't proving yourself but living life and being part of the human family; when you understand this, your ability to achieve is enhanced because your energy can be 100% directed toward life. You can be less afraid of failure and willing to take more risks. You can be less defensive because you don't have to defend your ego and your worth. You can enjoy life more because your energy won't go into neurotic worrying about being good enough. Instead of worrying about your worth, you can concentrate on living fully. You can discover unexpected opportunities for every aspect of life that counts. Indeed, the best self-concept is none at all.

The first step on the path to psychological health is a commitment to living and to being our true self. The more we replace the desire to rise above mankind with an appreciation of being part of mankind, the easier life becomes. The more unrealistically grandiose our self-image and our self-presentation, the more susceptible we are to insecurity and fear of failure. The more we align with others, rather than seeing others as competition and a threat, the world becomes less hostile and we become less susceptible to fear and anxiety (the second obstacle to psychological health). Distortion of reality always causes more problems than it solves. We aren't more valuable or important than others; we aren't indispensable. Mere mortals that we are, our life will be neither easy nor fair; eventually, if not sooner, we will die. Any and all attempts to deny these realities only interfere with our ability to live effectively and with peace.

11 — *A Guide to Rational Living*, Third Edition, by Albert Ellis and Robert Harper (Hollywood: Melvin Powers Wilshire Book Company, 1997), p. 126.

12 — See *Ten Days to Self-Esteem*, by David Burns (New York: William Morrow and Company, 1993) or *Self-Esteem*, Third Edition, by Matthew McKay and Patrick Fanning (Oakland: New Harbinger Publications, 2000).

13 — *A Guide to Rational Living*, Third Edition, by Albert Ellis and Robert Harper (Hollywood: Melvin Powers Wilshire Book Company, 1997).

14 — *Don't Sweat the Small Stuff...and It's All Small Stuff*, by Richard Carlson (New York: Hyperion, 1997), p. 192. Reprinted by permission of Hyperion.

15 — *The Warrior Athlete*, by Dan Millman (Walpole, New Hampshire: Stillpoint Publishing, 1979), p. 50. Excerpted with written permission from Stillpoint Publishing.

16 — *Neurosis and Human Growth: The Struggle toward Self-Realization*, by Karen Horney (New York: W. W. Norton & Company, 1950), pp. 89-90.

17 — *The Greatest Miracle in the World*, by Og Mandino (New York: Bantam Books, 1975), p. 18.

Chapter THREE
OVERCOMING FEAR AND ANXIETY

It seems that the great general (Alexander the Great) was about to lead his army against a powerful foe whose men greatly outnumbered his own. Because of the odds against them, his army had shown little enthusiasm for the upcoming battle as they set sail for what they feared would be their end. When Alexander finally unloaded his men and equipment on enemy shores he issued an order for all his ships to be burned. As their means of retreat slowly sank in flames behind them Alexander rose to address his men and said, "see your crafts going up in smoke, their ashes floating on the sea? That is our assurance that we shall be victorious for none of us can leave this despicable land unless we are victorious in battle. Men, when we go home we are going home in their ships!"

Og Mandino [18]

Something about life makes people afraid—maybe it's our mortality (the only certainty in life is death). Maybe it's the frailty of our bodies and how damage suffered often can never be repaired. It seems built in biologically: dogs, unfamiliar with stairs, will quiver and shake and refuse to go down—even though objectively there is no real danger. We humans even experience fear watching a scary movie even though we know it's only a movie.

Human fear includes more than a concern for our physical safety; we also fear for our emotional safety. Abraham Maslow, a deceased American psychologist, coined the term "the Jonah complex" to refer to people's fear of failure. People fear looking dumb or inadequate, they fear rejection. People have a powerful tendency to fear what others think of them and to be more concerned about that than about what is truly important in life. I joke with clients that what I think of them and 50 cents will get them a cup of coffee. I admit to them that I would like them as well as all my clients (and to be honest my neighbors, friends, and the world at large) to think that I am the greatest therapist on the face of the planet (as well as the best looking)—but I don't need that. It isn't as valuable as good health, a pay raise, or even how well or poorly the restaurant fixed my eggs for breakfast this morning. What others think of us isn't as important as we let it be. It makes little sense to fear looking stupid or being embarrassed to the extent most of us do.

People avoid making decisions because they fear making the wrong choice. People are reluctant to make changes because the unknown frightens them. People stay in terrible marriages because they are afraid to live and survive on their own. People stay in life circumstances such as jobs, professions, or living arrangements they dislike rather than make a change. People are reluctant to make changes because change involves risk—maybe the unknown will be worse than what they have. They stay with what they hate rather than risk the unknown. Even when people do make changes, they often take years to make that decision because of fear when it could and should have been done more quickly. Many people who reflect back on their life in later years realize that they wasted years because it took them too long to face problems and make decisions, that they were entirely too cautious— and their life was unnecessarily limited as a result.

I'm currently seeing a 35-year-old woman, Carrie. When Carrie first came for therapy she weighed 240 pounds (5'2"). She had never moved out from her parents. She didn't date. She had a phobia of driving on the freeway and avoided that totally. For the last 13 years, she had worked at the same job making $19,000 a year with no benefits. One of the few positive things she had done was to get her Associate's Degree in early childhood education. Her best friend owned a business and had offered her a job with substantially better pay and benefits, but she declined the offer in order to stay where she was comfortable. Her neurotic fear developed in part because of a critical, domineering, overprotective father who undermined her self-confidence and never encouraged her independence. She came to therapy for help with depression.

Carrie has responded well to therapy—as such clients do if they have the courage to face their fears. Besides getting her on Prozac through the staff psychiatrist, I have helped her to acknowledge and confront how afraid she had become of life. After 12 sessions over 6 months, she is starting to drive on the freeway, is discussing the other job with her friend, has lost 15 pounds, and is starting to talk with men at work. She is starting to think in terms of dating and moving out on her own. She is starting to get used to change. We're comfortable with something we do often; Carrie is getting less afraid of change because change is starting to become common in her life rather than something she avoids at all cost. The changes she needs to make are extensive and involve deeply engrained traits and habits; they will take considerable time—a year or more. But success is guaranteed as long as she continues to have the courage to face her fears and act despite them.

As the saying goes, the only thing in life that's constant is change. Being afraid of change leads to life becoming more and more confined and limited, more and more neurotic, more and more impossible. Depression often coexists with neurotic fear because withdrawing from life out of fear leads to a life devoid of joy, satisfaction, and meaning. Carrie's fearful avoidance of life understandably resulted in her being depressed. She would have paid a huge price for continuing to allow fear to dominate her life. That would have led to never marrying and having children; when her parents died she would have found herself alone and helpless. Why look upon change as a threat? Why expect the worst? Why not see change as an exciting opportunity for previously unforeseen possibilities?

Letting fear play too big a role is the most common and most destructive mistake people make in life. Fear plays a major role in our life, whether we are aware of it or not. Such traits as self-doubt, shyness, a reluctance to be assertive, needing the approval of others, difficulty making decisions, unwillingness to make changes all have fear as the underlying factor. Most fear fits one of the following basic types:

- Fear of death, illness, injury, pain or suffering

- Fear of the loss of something we want or need— financial security, job, house, spouse

- Fear of change, the unknown, uncertainty

- Fear of embarrassment, humiliation, failure

- Fear of fear—fear of the unpleasant symptoms of panic attacks or of anxiety

A certain amount of fear is healthy; otherwise, we would constantly and needlessly put ourselves at risk. I'm amazed at the risk some drivers take cutting in and out of traffic, driving over the speed limit in terrible driving conditions; this is an unhealthy lack of fear to the point of foolishness. But there's an even more prevalent tendency for fear to exceed reasonable healthy boundaries, for fear to interfere with our ability to live more than serve a functional protective role. Fear becomes neurotic when a person puts more energy into his defense mechanisms, more energy into protecting himself than he puts into living; when he becomes so afraid of life that fear interferes significantly with his ability to live. [19] And the important thing is to live, to take advantage of the wonderful opportunities life offers—rather than to hide from life. What's the worst that can happen, you're going to die anyway? This fear goes very deep. Even the mothering instinct promotes neurotic fear for many who otherwise might do fine—people who aren't afraid and worried for themselves but who worry tremendously regarding their children and grandchildren. Many people who avoid neurotic fear in regard to their own life lose all ability to trust life and people's ability to deal with life when it pertains to their children.

When fear is neurotic is a subjective judgment. A fear of snakes is unlikely to interfere with life at all; a fear of the dentist is likely to cause some problems; a fear of being around other people makes life almost impossible. A fear of flying might be inconsequential for a North Dakota farmer but have severe consequences for a salesman whose job involves international sales. A fear of flying, of driving on the freeway, of bungee jumping represents far greater potential danger than a fear of spiders or a fear of crowded places. Neurotic fear commonly pertains to perceived psychological danger as opposed to perceived physical danger because physical danger is more real and catastrophic than psychological danger (a plane crash versus looking foolish), and fear of physical danger is less limiting in scope than fear of psychological danger (the fear of flying versus the fear of what others think). In addition, what appears to be fear of physical danger often is fear of psychological danger (a fear of appearing childish rather than a fear of dental pain).

Trying to avoid and escape fear is like trying to avoid death or taxes; it can't be done. Resisting, avoiding, or running from fear at the time may seem like the safe course; but in the long run it's anything but safe—the fear will become stronger in intensity and may well become broader in scope. Give in to fear too much and your fears may become more and more irrational rather than merely the normal fears that have to be accepted as part of life. Anyone learning they have cancer or some other life-threatening health problem understandably will experience fear. But triskaidekaphobia, the fear of the number 13—how much sense does that make? Yet high-rise hotels frequently eliminate the thirteenth floor in their numbering systems, and some people actually schedule plane flights so as to avoid Friday the thirteenth. If you give in to fear, your life will move from the fears that are unavoidably part of life to others that are unnecessary and sometimes even ludicrous. And, as your fears become more inclusive, your life will become more restricted. Giving in to fear becomes a habit and always leads to limiting your life.

Courage isn't the absence of fear, but the willingness to act despite fear. Fear is an inescapable, inevitable factor in life, but we don't have to let it take over our life. We all have neurotic tendencies, but we don't have to be neurotic. We can accept the fact that life is dangerous and make an agreement with ourselves to act despite fear. This is the only way we can fully live.

Anxiety is our internal reaction to fear; it is manifested by the following physical symptoms: muscle tension, feeling shaky, cold or clammy hands, dry mouth, sweating, nausea, diarrhea, urinary frequency, trouble swallowing, being easily startled, restlessness or feeling on edge. When fear becomes particularly intense the corresponding level of anxiety may escalate into "panic" which is manifested by the following physical symptoms (in addition to the basic anxiety symptoms listed above): accelerated heart rate, shortness of breath, chest pain or discomfort, feeling dizzy or lightheaded, numbness or tingling sensations, chills or hot flushes.

Anxiety disorders are the leading mental health disorder among American women and second to only drug and alcohol abuse among men. Thirty million Americans suffer from anxiety disorders every year (compared to 19 million with depression), with only a small portion receiving treatment. Five percent of Americans at some time in their life suffer Generalized Anxiety Disorder (excessive anxiety and worry occurring most of the time). Two percent of Americans have panic attacks, 10% have one or more phobia that interferes significantly in their life, 8% suffer Social Phobia (pronounced anxiety about being embarrassed or looking foolish in social interactions). While genetic factors make some people more susceptible to anxiety and panic, fear plays a significant role in the development and continuation of all anxiety. While fear plays a role in everyone's life, it plays a particularly significant role in the life of people with anxiety disorders.

Fear can only be overcome with action. If someone is afraid of going to the dentist, the longer he or she puts that off the stronger the fear will become. Psychologists no longer treat anxiety disorders through psychoanalysis; years on the couch talking about your childhood may help you understand how you got to be such a coward, but it will do little to make you brave. Rather, we treat anxiety disorders with exposure techniques—systematic desensitization, flooding, or some combination of both. You can deal with your own fears and anxiety in a similar fashion.

Systematic desensitization is the process of overcoming fear step-by-step. You can make the steps as small as necessary and progress from one to the next at whatever pace you choose. If you had a phobia of snakes, you could set up the following action plan: read and learn about snakes, watch a film of snakes, watch a snake handler, hold a tiny harmless snake, hold a slightly larger snake, and so on. With systematic desensitization, if the fear becomes pronounced you can withdraw and go back to the activity or situation later; the important point is that you continue exposing yourself to the fear and the feared object or activity, that you keep practicing such exposure until you get more comfortable—and thus less anxious.

The flooding technique involves something like going into a snake den with a snake handler and staying there, watching him handle snakes and then doing it yourself, until you have a greatly reduced or nonexistent fear of snakes. With flooding it's crucial that you remain in the anxiety-producing situation until the anxiety has resolved itself—you agree to expose yourself to the feared activity or situation and to remain there and let happen whatever happens. In the example given, you don't leave the snake den when the anxiety gets intense; you stay until the anxiety lessens—and anxiety has to lessen eventually (our systems can't stay on red-alert indefinitely). The two approaches can also be combined on the same problem. A person with a fear of heights (acrophobia) could go to the fifteenth floor of the highest building around and stay until the anxiety subsided (flooding). Then he could step-by-step, floor-by-floor, work on his fear of the higher floors (systematic desensitization).

People prefer systematic desensitization techniques over flooding because the latter demands a great deal of courage, but flooding can save a great deal of time—and few things in life are more valuable than time. Someone with a phobia of driving on the freeway, for example, might spend months, if not longer, overcoming that phobia with systematic desensitization—depending on how protective he is of himself. But this person could overcome his phobia in a week or less if he drove on the freeway daily for hours at a time. Doing that might even lead to becoming bored or irritated—rather than anxious. In dealing with your own fears, consider flooding techniques so as to not lose more time to fear than absolutely necessary.

The exposure techniques (systematic desensitization and flooding) involve exposing yourself both to the activity, object, or situation feared and to the uncomfortable feeling of anxiety that accompanies fear. Stay with the uncomfortable feeling—accept it, float, let time pass. If you do, the fear and anxiety will diminish or go away entirely. If you don't, the fear and anxiety will get worse. Be willing to experience anxiety; become comfortable with that unpleasant feeling. One of the paradoxical aspects of fear and anxiety is that acceptance of them leads to becoming comfortable and no longer afraid or anxious; whereas if you fight or run from them, they become worse. If you believe and act as if fear and anxiety are dreadful, the worst or most embarrassing things that could happen, you only intensify them. Another method which doesn't work is to put on a false front and pretend to yourself and others you are not afraid; accept and acknowledge and let others see your fear— but they will also see, and you will know, that you are brave enough to act despite that fear.

Ironically and paradoxically, people often inadvertently cause what they are afraid of. People with panic attacks become so afraid of having more attacks that they increase the likelihood of another attack. If a man is afraid he won't be able to perform sexually, that fear is likely to interfere with normal sexual functioning and cause impotency. (This fear is anything but sexually stimulating; sexuality is a powerful drive but amidst great danger people are unlikely to get sexually stimulated by anyone or anything.) As a matter of fact, the treatment approaches for impotency developed by Masters and Johnson had the couple engage in sexual play, but intercourse was forbidden. Now, with no need for an erection, the fear of failure hopefully was bypassed and the couple would take advantage of the result and disobey the injunction against intercourse. The fear of failure makes failure more likely because fear affects our body and our mind and interferes with their natural functioning. The person with a fear of giving a talk or presentation may be distracted by his fearful thoughts and forget what he was saying or thinking. A method used to counteract this pattern is to visualize and imagine a desired positive outcome (e.g. the ball landing on the green); among the benefits of this method is the interruption of the mind's destructive fear of failure.

As seen in the last chapter, the more we feel connected to the family of man, rather than needing to assert our superiority, the less hostile the world seems and the less susceptible we are to fear and anxiety. In addition, being too preoccupied with self leads to being self-conscious which in turn makes us more susceptible to fear and anxiety. People are too busy to notice or be preoccupied with you and your anxiety; they're more concerned about their own life circumstances, even what they're having for dinner tonight. And in neurotic fear and self-preoccupation, people become detached and disinterested in the world at large. The agoraphobic mother who can't drive rushes her injured child to the emergency room because her child's injury reconnects her to the importance of life; it shifts her focus from herself to something outside herself, something that needs to be done. Psychologically healthy people have interests and care about other people; they are more committed to life and living than preoccupied and fearful regarding their own safety.

The following remarks regarding shyness by David Reynolds (summarizing the ideas of Japanese psychiatrist Shoma Morita, M. D. some 100 years ago) reflect these universal and timeless truths regarding fear and anxiety:

> *While accepting the reality of your shyness, go on doing what you need to do in life. That means in spite of quivering knees and pounding heart, call that guy or gal you'd like to know better, tell your boss you'd do better work if he didn't stand at your shoulder all the time, make that speech, do the shopping in that crowded store. Call, tell, make, do—those are all actions. Get on about living even though you are shy. Paradoxically, the more you do these things, the less shy you will feel. Not only will you become more skillful and confident in social situations by gaining experience in them (no one ever became a good golfer just by watching) but you will be turning more and more attention away from yourself (and your own problems) toward the reality out there....*

> *I am not suggesting that you deny or ignore your anxieties. I am saying that going on about your business of living, bringing your attention back to the tasks at hand (the requirements of the situation), will result in the pleasant side effect of less shyness. Someday, with much practice, it absolutely will not matter to you whether you are feeling shy or not. You'll be able to make the date, make the speech, do the shopping, propose, demand, refuse, whatever, however you are feeling at the time. That's the secret of overcoming shyness. It is*

really overcoming the interference of shyness in daily life. That's what maturity is all about—not feeling confident all the time but doing what needs doing regardless of your feelings. Incidentally, the shy feelings will eventually fade—you just won't have time for the self-indulgence of noticing them. You'll be too busy living. [20]

A therapy technique that can be useful in dealing with fear involves continuing to ask the client "and then what?" Often people don't specify their fears so they never get the chance to recognize that the feared event wouldn't be as devastating as they assume. Someone with a fear of public speaking would be led to specify exactly what he or she is afraid of. Forgetting what to say, stuttering, or turning bright red boil down to the fear of being embarrassed, of looking foolish or stupid, of being humiliated. The therapist continues to ask "and then what?" Most of us could live with that. The world wouldn't end; our dog would still greet us every night when we get home. I remind clients that no one likes to look foolish but how awful would that be—compared to testicular cancer or having your child die? Taking a closer look at our fears generally reveals we wouldn't like the event we fear, but we could live with it; it wouldn't be as devastating as we assume when we don't specify what we're afraid of. This is particularly true when our fears involve psychological rather than physical outcomes or events. Albert Ellis, Ph. D. developed "shame attacking exercises" as a technique for dealing with this phobic concern with being humiliated. The person afraid of embarrassment or humiliation does something embarrassing or humiliating so he can experience and discover that this isn't as catastrophic as he thought—like carrying a sign that says "I'm stupid," lying down on the floor at a mall, or wearing an outfit that is hopelessly out of style or outlandish.

The fear of fear that occurs in Panic Disorder might be difficult for readers to understand. Panic symptoms (as listed above) are unpleasant enough that people come to fear their occurrence (just as someone else might fear looking foolish or losing his job). Then, as always, the fear is likely to cause the symptoms feared. People with panic attacks need to be reminded that, while a panic attack is unpleasant, nothing catastrophic results from one. No one dies of a panic attack (contrary to the frequent trips to the emergency room made by some people with panic attacks); a person with a panic attack can still drive his car (even though he feels as though he couldn't). The more people understand the role their own fear plays in the intensity and continuance of their panic, the more likely they are to develop more effective methods of responding. Similar to people with Panic Disorder, people with anxiety need to learn effective ways to manage and cope with their anxiety symptoms and hence to be less afraid of them (see the ideas presented in Chapter One: The Art of Being Unreasonably Happy). Our natural tendency to freeze, quit breathing, tense up, or flee (the fight or flight response) doesn't work in our complex modern world. Being willing to act despite fear and anxiety, based upon unconditional acceptance of life, is more effective.

There are two tendencies behind anxiety: (1) the tendency to exaggerate the likelihood of something bad happening, and (2) the tendency to underestimate our ability to deal with it if it does happen. It's common for people to spend time and energy worrying about problems or disasters that never happen; the feared disaster doesn't ruin their life but the anxiety and worry does. And when bad things do happen, people generally find some way to cope; people deal with divorce, bankruptcy, health problems, all types of tragedy. We don't even need to be afraid of death—and it's important to overcome this fear because not only will we die, we know we will die. One cannot overcome a neurotic fear of life until one has a comfortableness and acceptance of one's own mortality (see Chapter Eleven).

Earlier this week I saw Katherine, age 61, for the first time. Unfortunately she waited this long to come for psychotherapy—despite a life dominated by neurotic fear. With a history of panic attacks, she has lived life "terrified of heart problems." She has been to the emergency room dozens of times, has had numerous EKG's and Holter Monitor tests—always with normal results. She has avoided exercise or even carrying heavy objects—anything that might raise her heart rate. As chronic and entrenched as her neurotic fear is, I expect therapy to be successful within 8-10 sessions. In this initial session, I challenged her with: "Why are you so afraid of death?" "Why are you so afraid of a heart attack or stroke?" She left this first session with some confidence that she could face her fear of heart problems and focus more on living while she has the opportunity.

More important than how long you live, is how you live. It's important to live with zest and gusto rather than being afraid of life. It's better to make a mistake with courage than to hide from life and to be afraid to live. Former President Theodore Roosevelt commented:

The credit belongs to the man who is actually

*in the arena, who strives valiantly; who knows
the great enthusiasms, the great devotions, and
spends himself in a worthy cause; who at the
best, knows the triumph of high achievement;
and who, at worst, if he fails, at least fails while
daring greatly so that his place shall never be
with those cold and timid souls who know
neither victory nor defeat.*

Do an inventory of the role fear plays in your life.
Look closely at the fears you have and examine
whether or not they warrant the time, energy, and
concern you give them. Challenge fear when the only
danger is psychological. Be willing to make decisions;
if they turn our poorly, you can then decide what to
do about that. Take reasonable chances, make
changes, try new things. Don't spend time trying to
get rid of fear; learn to act despite fear. Acknowledge
your fear but do exactly what you would do if you
weren't afraid. Be willing to ask that woman for a date,
accept the invitation to give that speech or
presentation, ask your boss for what you want. You
commonly pay a price for being afraid to do so; as
the saying goes "Nothing ventured, nothing gained."
You let many possibilities in life pass you by if you're
unwilling to take risk. "I can't" almost always means
"I won't, I'm afraid to." Only action overcomes fear.
Acting despite fear starts to become something you
become used to; and, as a result, starts to become
easier and less frightening.

Fear is a hurdle that must be overcome; failure to
do so makes life impossible. As Helen Keller stated:
"Security is mostly a superstition. It does not exist in
nature, nor do the children of men as a whole
experience it. Avoiding danger is no safer in the long

run than outright exposure. Life is either a daring adventure, or nothing." Despite your fear and uncertainty, give life a try. Be willing to look foolish, to care little about the approval of others, to fail. Your greatest confidence should exist in knowing you are willing to act despite fear and anxiety. There is nothing wrong with fear—as long as you don't allow that fear to intrude upon what needs to be done in your daily life. Live life bravely rather than hiding from life out of cowardliness and fear; if you do you will feel more alive, more invigorated, and happier.

Chapter Three Notes

18 — *The Greatest Miracle in the World*, by Og Mandino (New York: Bantam Books, 1975), p. 52.

19 — Anxiety, which results from fear, has long been acknowledged in psychological theory as the most significant factor underlying neurosis.

20 — *Constructive Living*, by David Reynolds (Honolulu: University of Hawaii Press, 1984), pp. 35-37.

Chapter FOUR
BE FLEXIBLE—BE BALANCED

I was lecturing in Memphis, Tennessee, and my host and hostess attended. At the end of the lecture, the hostess remarked, "The lecture lasted rather long, so let's eat at a restaurant. We know a very nice French restaurant. My husband and I have dined there twice a week for 25 years."

I looked upon that statement as entirely pathological. To eat at the same restaurant in Memphis, where there are a lot of restaurants... to eat at the same one twice a week for 25 years...so I agreed.

Of course, having my suspicions, I ordered escargots. And the way they looked at me as I ate my snails. When I was down to one snail, I persuaded my host to taste it. He ate it and said, "That's good." So then I persuaded his wife to taste it and she found it good. So I ordered my second order of escargots. They ordered their first order, and they enjoyed it.

Six months later, I was in Memphis, lecturing and they were again my hosts. The lecture lasted late and my hostess said, "Instead of having dinner at home, let's go to a restaurant. We know a very nice German restaurant, or would you prefer some other type? There is a

catfish restaurant that is very nice." She offered
me several other choices. Since they mentioned
the German restaurant, I went there with them.
Halfway through the meal, I turned to my host
and said, "By the way, when was the last time
you went to that French restaurant?" He said,
"I don't know, six weeks, two months. Honey,
when did we go last to that French restaurant?"
She said, "Oh, I think about two months ago."
   After 25 years, twice a week...(Erickson
laughs)... that was pathological.

Milton H. Erickson, M. D. [21]

W e tend to be creatures of habit. Many people do go to the same one or two restaurants over and over. This makes life easier, more predictable, safer—you don't have difficulty finding the restaurant, don't end up with food you can't stand, and probably get treated well because of being a regular customer. Going to the same restaurant time and again seems so insignificant and innocent it might puzzle readers that a renowned therapy expert would label doing so as pathological. As a matter of fact, people routinely develop and resort to such habitual behavior. In doing group therapy, it strikes me how most clients sit in the same place week after week. Again this makes life easier, more predictable, safer—you don't have to decide each time where to sit, you've already introduced yourself to the person next to you, you won't end up in an uncomfortable chair or next to someone obnoxious. Again this seems insignificant and innocent. In both situations, people know what to expect—there's something comforting about that.

There is a downside, however, to habitually doing the same thing. The longer we do that, the more uncomfortable we become doing otherwise. After sitting in the same place long enough, there's a tendency to feel uneasy about sitting somewhere else, even though that makes no logical sense. After eating the same kind of food at the same restaurant long enough, there's a tendency to feel uneasy about eating other kinds of food or going to other restaurants. As we saw in Chapter Three, the fear of change, of the unknown, of uncertainty is one of the prevalent categories of human fear. Even if fear is not a factor in our initially engaging in such a habit pattern, it eventually becomes a factor. If we refrain from doing something long enough, we become anxious about doing it. The longer we go without trying new foods, meeting new people, driving on the freeway, living anywhere other than Cleveland the more uncomfortable we become in doing so.

It gets worse. A person who is rigid and inflexible in one area is prone to become that way in others; the more we avoid new things, the more that becomes a pattern. Rigidity and inflexibility becomes a habit; we become uncomfortable with change in general. Being afraid of change leads to life becoming more and more confined and limited. Uncomfortable with anything outside our normal patterns, as our habit patterns multiply there are more and more things we can't any longer do. We end up no longer able to explore other alternatives. Our habit patterns put us at risk for ever-increasing rigidity to the point of diminishing our effectiveness in dealing with life. The popular television show *All in the Family* portrayed the danger involved with becoming set and rigid in what one does and in how one does things. Archie Bunker always sat in the same chair, he only ate certain foods and always at the same time. After years of such behavior, Archie had many things he simply couldn't do—dance, be affectionate in public, go to the opera, eat anything other than standard American food. He became rigid in his beliefs and attitudes; he became incapable of keeping an open mind if someone was Black or Hispanic, lesbian or homosexual, had long hair or dressed differently.

Flexibility is essential for mental health, for living effectively; it allows one to use a wide range of approaches rather than responding in one set manner. Different situations, different circumstances, warrant different responses; healthy people are able to vary their approach according to what is appropriate and most effective for each situation. Unhealthy people compulsively respond to situations in some set way, whether or not that approach is appropriate or effective. They are incapable of responding otherwise. Some people are always meek and unassertive; others always respond forcefully or even aggressively. Some people always think only of themselves; others are incapable of acting for their own needs. The healthy person has amazing flexibility in dealing with life in all its complexities, with the result that he is free to respond in any particular situation in the manner most appropriate for that situation rather than being forced to respond in the only manner in which he or she any longer feels comfortable. Archie Bunker never realized how little choice he had in what he did and how he reacted; much of the humor involved the audience's ability to foresee and predict his response—even though he didn't have a clue. The compulsive nature of these drives inevitably deprives the person of his autonomy and spontaneity; his responses become absolutely predictable. Such people commonly are totally unaware of the difference between wanting (being the driver) and being compulsively driven.

The healthy person lives with choice and self-determination rather than being compelled by factors beyond his conscious awareness. Compulsivity, in all aspects and forms, is contrary to mental health; it is one of the prominent aspects of neurosis. Most, if not all, psychiatric disturbance essentially comes down to this factor. It's good to wash your hands, but being compelled to wash your hands hundreds of times a day isn't. It's good to have concern regarding what you eat; but in eating disorders like bulimia and anorexia this concern loses balance and becomes problematic, sometimes even leading to death. I'm currently seeing an 18-year-old woman in therapy who is 5'4" and weighs 102 pounds. She won't eat anything with any significant amount of fat, calories, or sugar. She eats the same empty 3 meals every day—weighing everything she eats and spending at least an hour a day calculating her daily calories over and over. If she eats anything outside these rigid limits, she forces herself to throw up (something she does 3 to 4 times a week). Not very healthy.

All therapists see "hoarders," people who compulsively keep every item that could prove useful regardless of how remote the likelihood it will be needed or its value or importance if needed. Their houses, basements, garages, sheds become more and more impossible to live in—with paths through the madness and sticky notes everywhere trying to keep order. Eventually they wouldn't be able to find something even if it were needed. They come for therapy because their life has become impossible—and yet they absolutely can't throw anything away. They know that their behavior makes no sense, that it limits their life and their ability to live; yet they cannot change what they are doing—it has become such an ingrained habit. And when they try to change, it takes them hours to go through one stack of papers, days to go through one room. They find themselves unable to change the real problem—even in thinking that they are making progress, they maintain the same cautious attitude that every scrap of paper might be a matter of life or death. They may manage to throw out or give away a few items; what they need to get rid of is their neurotic inability to trust that if they need something in life that they don't have, they'll find some way to cope or get by. Their behavior has become too rigid, too set, too compulsive for them to any longer make a rational free choice.

The personality disorders, one of the largest groups of mental health disorders, are long-standing, inflexible patterns of perceiving, interpreting, and responding to one's environment and to oneself that are characteristic of the individual's functioning across a wide range of situations. The incidence of people with these inflexible personality patterns is high—an estimated 50% of the adult population. Paranoid Personality Disorder people lose the ability to trust others. Schizoid Personality Disorder people lose the ability to enjoy social relationships. Dependent Personality Disorder people lose the ability to function without someone to depend on. Narcissistic Personality Disorder people lose the ability to care about and value others. Obsessive-Compulsive Personality Disorder people become perfectionistic and preoccupied with order and rules and lose the ability to enjoy life. Codependent Personality Disorder people (the parent who can't throw out their 30-year-old verbally abusive alcoholic son who doesn't work and has children he doesn't support) take caring for and protecting others to excess and lose the ability to care about their own wants and needs. There are other personality disorders, but they all lack flexibility in some important manner.

Many other mental health disorders are caused at least in part by rigidity. Over 50% of clients presenting with depression have significant personality disorder traits (the inability to be assertive, excessively needing other's approval, perfectionism) that play a role in the disorder and require attention in any successful treatment approach. Alcoholics are notoriously rigid in personality style and behavior. Besides becoming rigid in what they do and in their personality traits, people become rigid in their way of thinking about the world, their beliefs and attitudes, their moods. Angry people see things that make them angry, depressed people see depressing things, anxious people see frightening things more often than people without these traits. Rigidity develops into compulsivity and loss of choice—with regard not only to what you do, but your personality traits, how you feel, what you think.

Be careful of the things you can't do, or can't avoid doing. You have a problem if you're always losing your temper, never able to stand up for what you want or need, have difficulty being playful, or can't get along without a drink. As a therapist, I'm concerned about what a particular individual, couple, or family can't do. There are people whose life is ruined because they are too lazy to work, just as there are people whose life is ruined because they are workaholics (they can't not work). There are people who can't be sexual, just as there are people whose life is totally driven by their out-of-control sexuality. There are families that can't be physically affectionate, couples where the man always has to be in charge. Some people can't enjoy parties; others can't do anything other than party. Some people can't be organized; others have to be totally organized. None of this is healthy. The healthy person even takes things which are viewed as opposites and mutually exclusive, and is able to do both. The healthy person can be hard driving and intense when that is appropriate; but easy going, laid back, and casual when that is appropriate. He or she can be independent in one circumstance and time and utterly dependent in another. He can be altruistic and concerned about other people and at the same time concerned about himself and his own needs.

Rigidity loses a quality meant to add balance. The codependent person is out of balance (compulsively sacrificing his own needs for the needs of someone else or taking more responsibility for someone than that person takes for himself); he loses the ability to care about and value himself. Narcissists lose the ability to care about and value others. Workaholics lose the ability to play, have fun, be intimate. Perfectionists lose the ability to relax and enjoy life. Healthy people are balanced. They can be comfortable and enjoy being alone as well as being with others. They are comfortable being in charge but don't need to be in charge. They can act for their own wants and needs; yet are able to sacrifice that for the wants and needs of others when they so choose. They are able to get angry; yet able to restrain their anger out of love and compassion.

On virtually all issues, being out of balance to either extreme is unhealthy. I have seen clients who are driven to have sex 3 to 4 times a day and clients who, without any good reason, have avoided sexuality for years; both are unhealthy. Abstaining from sexuality as a conscious choice for a specific reason (a priest or monk choosing to be celibate or someone who believes that sex is immoral outside marriage) is not psychologically unhealthy—although such a person may have difficulty being sexually well adjusted. Being too lazy to work or being a workaholic are both unhealthy. Other examples of diametrically opposed ways of being out of balance, and thus unhealthy, include: being selfish or being incapable of acting for one's own needs, being uncomfortable around people or not being able to tolerate being alone, being unassertive or being domineering and aggressive, being unable to play and have fun or being unable to do something unless it's fun.

Even qualities that are positive and valuable become problematic if one becomes rigid and extreme in that regard. There are things in life one has to be able to do to live effectively and be happy (work, play, be intimate and sexual, be assertive, be organized, be disciplined). But these all need to be kept in balance; otherwise, you just have a different problem. Any quality, regardless of how valuable, becomes a problem and a flaw if taken to the extreme. People's unique qualities blossom into wonderful assets under the umbrella of flexibility; they turn poisonous and deadly in the atmosphere of rigidity.

Ironically, the more rigid and compulsive a person becomes, the less awareness he tends to have regarding his rigidity and compulsivity. As a result those who most need psychotherapy, or help from some other source, frequently lack insight into that need. Archie Bunker would have been the last person to admit or recognize that there was anything wrong with him or his approach to life.

In considering change, people worry about going from one extreme on an issue to the opposite extreme; this never happens. People who lack sexual drive and interest never become out-of-control sex fiends. People who are lazy and unable to work never become workaholics. People who are unassertive don't become aggressive, bullying, domineering. There are people who are assertive in one area of life, like at work, who lack healthy assertiveness in another area, like romantic relationships. But even then, with regard to any particular area of life they never go from one extreme to the other; such a person is unlikely to become unassertive at work or domineering in romantic relationships. In considering change, you don't have to worry about going too far in the opposite direction. What you do need to worry about, what does pose great threat is becoming too rigidly the way you are. The person who has a low sex drive may lose all interest in sex. The person who is a good worker and provider over the years may become a workaholic. The person who is assertive may become domineering and controlling.

Commitment to values and beliefs requires balance. It's healthy to have political views, religious values, cultural and ethnic pride; but values and beliefs can become rigid and extreme to the point of psychological disturbance, racism, and prejudice. Life is too complex to be one hundred percent certain of most things; extreme views reflect a neurotic need to see the world as more clear-cut than it actually is. There are republicans and democrats who have contempt for anyone "naïve" enough to endorse the opposite political view. There are people on both sides of the abortion issue who view those with the opposing view as contemptible (even to the extreme of bombing abortion clinics). Some people feel so strongly about the death penalty that they regard anyone with the opposite view as stupid. Adolf Hitler believed strongly in Arian supremacy. When I grew up Catholic, we were taught that only Catholics could go to heaven; many religions, including Catholicism, have become psychologically healthier by abandoning such intolerant, holier-than-thou attitudes. Healthy people avoid a smarter-than-thou attitude; they have beliefs and values they support, but they are humble and healthy enough to know that other people might legitimately disagree. They are reluctant to force their values or beliefs on others, particularly through violence. Being too adamant, even contemptuous of the opposing view is out of balance and pathological. Richard Carlson, Ph. D. suggests writing down your 5 most rigid positions and then seeing if you can soften them. He states, "It doesn't make you weak to soften your positions. In fact, it makes you stronger." [22] Healthy people have even been known on occasion to change their opinion.

Healthy people try to maintain a balance in their personal life. They take time for themselves, their relationship with their significant other, their children. In the real world, however, often there is insufficient time to cater to all three areas; many people then sacrifice their own needs or those of their relationship for the needs of their children. This may be necessary and healthy, but it is unfortunate and dangerous— especially if taken to extremes. In the long run the children may suffer as well—either as a result of a chronically unhappy parent or divorce.

Another aspect of being balanced is having a wide range of interests and hobbies. Healthy people are able to put a tremendous amount of time and energy into any given activity, but they have a wide range of things they do—or at least would love to do if they had the time. They can read, dance, be athletic, be intimate and sexual, play golf, go to the ballet, travel. Healthy people are interested in life, including life's many and varied aspects. Sports gets a bad rap in this regard. There's nothing wrong with being intensely interested in sports (that can be a valuable interest that can add to one's life); it only becomes a problem when the person isn't interested in anything except sports. Gymnastics is an activity that adds value to one's life in various ways, but the young protégé who spends endless hours in gymnastics training is at risk for missing other aspects of life that are equally valuable. The problem isn't the time spent in the designated activity; it's the time that doesn't get spent in other areas—the resulting lack of balance.

This book, like all psychological self-help books, is not meant to replace therapy. Nonetheless, this chapter can provide the framework, and at least a good starting point, for self-therapy. Effective self-therapy begins with the ability to perceive what important thing you can't do, what flaw or weakness is blocking your ability to live more effectively or to be happier. Life works as well as your biggest flaw or weakness. You can be a great person; but your life will be ruined if you are alcoholic, too lazy to work, aren't able to be intimate, can't care about and love others. Be honest and courageous—what are your major flaws (the things you can't do or can't avoid doing)? Are there areas or aspects of life where you're badly out of balance? Are there ways in which you've become rigid and inflexible—in your behavior, your beliefs and attitudes, your way of perceiving reality, your personality traits? Change any of those and you will be healthier psychologically and life will work better. Honesty and courage should enable you to identify the changes that need to be made (you can solicit feedback if necessary from those who know you best). If you don't know how, or aren't able to make those changes, seek professional psychological help.

To facilitate change, rather than identifying something as bad and therefore needing to be eliminated, it works better to add the corresponding valuable quality, trait, or behavior. The workaholic will have little success trying to convince himself work isn't that important; he will find it easier to change by thinking in terms of learning the value of fun, being playful, intimacy, enjoying the process of life. The codependent person will do better by learning to care about his own wants and needs than by trying to care less about others. The gymnastic protégé will be helped immensely by becoming interested in dating or some other activity. It works better to concentrate on developing the corresponding valuable habit or behavior you haven't yet acquired than to concentrate on eradicating a destructive habit or behavior.

Having looked at the major components of neurosis (egocentricity, fear and anxiety, and compulsivity rather than choice), we look next at another aspect of neurosis—distortion of reality.

21 — Copyright 1980 from *A Teaching Seminar* with Milton H. Erickson by Jeffrey Zeig (Editor), (New York: Brunner/Mazel Publishers, 1980), pp.253-254. Reproduced by permission of Routledge/Taylor & Francis Books, Inc.

22 — *Don't Sweat the Small Stuff...and It's All Small Stuff,* by Richard Carlson (New York: Hyperion, 1997), p. 125. Reprinted by permission of Hyperion.

Chapter FIVE
DON'T EXPECT LIFE TO BE FAIR

> We are conditioned to look for justice in life and when
> it doesn't appear, we tend to feel anger, anxiety, or
> frustration. Actually, it would be equally productive to
> search for the fountain of youth, or some such myth.
> Justice does not exist. It never has, it never will. The
> world is simply not put together that way. Robins eat
> worms. That's not fair to worms.... You have only to
> look at nature to realize there is no justice in the world.
> Tornadoes, floods, tidal waves, droughts are all unfair.
> Dr. Wayne Dyer [23]

Throughout my childhood and adolescence
growing up on a farm in Southwestern
Wisconsin, whenever there were violent
thunderstorms and the threat of tornadoes, my very
catholic mother ushered the family into the basement
to recite the rosary before a votive candle. These
storms seemed to occur most often during the middle
of the night as if some cosmic force delighted in this
ritualistic sacrifice of my sleep (even throughout
adolescence there was nothing optional about this
practice). Well our lives were spared (along with the
house, barn, cows, and family dogs); and we, my
mother in particular, were comforted to know God
protects and looks after those who pray for his help.
It was a simple but good life and everything seemed

right with the world.

As an adult I have lived in Wisconsin, Minnesota, Missouri, California, Illinois, Florida, and Ohio—mainly in large cities like Cleveland, San Diego, or Chicago; or in relatively large cities like Pensacola (Florida), Madison (Wisconsin), or San Bernardino (California). It strikes me people are much the same in those locations as we were on our little farm in Wisconsin during my childhood. I continue to see people praying for protection against life's storms—that their plane won't crash, that their children will enjoy good health, that their country will remain strong and free. It seems to work pretty well—most planes don't crash, most children enjoy good health, America remains strong and free.

Our beliefs, including our religious beliefs, sometimes are simplistic; and, as a result, lead to psychological problems—guilt, depression, rage, jealousy, self pity. Rabbi Harold Kushner, faced with the gut-wrenching life and death of his 14-year-old son from the rare "rapid aging" disease, wrote the national best-seller *When Bad Things Happen to Good People*.[24] Rabbi Kushner points out the flaws in the common belief that God gives people what they deserve: it doesn't fit the facts, it creates guilt when there is no basis for guilt, it leads people to distrust and hate God. It's comforting to believe that a fair, just, and loving God decides what is allowed to happen in our life—as long as everything goes well. But what are we to conclude when our child dies of some painful, prolonged illness as happened to Rabbi Kushner? Now that belief isn't so comforting—it means that our child deserved what happened; that we deserve our horrendous pain, loss, and suffering; that God is a punishing God more than a loving, forgiving God.

The belief that God, in his infinite wisdom, sees to it that people get what they deserve doesn't stand up to scrutiny. I see young mothers left widows with two or three young children who will grow up without a father. I see women who were the victim of sexual abuse as preadolescents. I see people with Alzheimer's who my clinical sense suggests were undeserving of such a fate. The truth is there is a totally unfair distribution of pain and suffering; innocent people have horrible things happen that destroy their life beyond repair. As a psychologist I have seen more people than I care to remember who were good people in every sense of that term, who nonetheless suffered unbearable loss and suffering. If God is in charge of these events, what sense can we make of anything? There are flaws in all our attempts to explain life's pain and suffering. Suffering often does not make people better; often people are destroyed by events with no chance to be better. If tragedy is a test, it often is a test people fail. It is unsatisfying to say suffering leads to a better next life; this is the life we know and this is the life we need to make sense of.

The unfair distribution of suffering is so much a part of life it should be obvious to everyone. It isn't possible to justify much of what happens in life as fair or as serving some noble cause. The reality is that life is neither fair nor unfair—it just happens. When a plane crashes, the good people on board die just as do the bad people. There are unscrupulous, derelict alcoholics who enjoy excellent health into their elderly years and innocent infants and children who die for no explainable reason. Reprehensible, despicable people have as good a chance of winning the lottery as you or I. People deny these obvious facts out of fear and insecurity. It's comforting to view life as fair.

This belief provides us with protection from life's calamities like a cosmic insurance package; it keeps the world orderly, understandable, and safe.

Religion sometimes is used to comfort neurotic fears and insecurity. It's comforting to believe God controls everything in the world and sees to it that people get what they deserve. Then, if one is reasonably moral and good, one can expect to be protected from those scary, horrendous things that happen in life. If you believe in God, let it be a mature concept of God, not a God who answers my prayers to be healed and yet decides that an innocent child should die a prolonged painful death of cancer. It defies any sensible concept of God to view him as causing the incredible undeserved pain and suffering that sometimes happens. Rabbi Kushner concluded that God does not cause our suffering; he does not cause the bad things that happen to us. He doesn't decide who will suffer misfortune and who will be spared. Life happens randomly according to the laws of nature and random events. God does not send us the problems; he gives us the strength to cope with them. It made some sense when my mother marched us to the basement because the basement is a good place to be during a tornado. And the votive candle may have been useful if the lights went out. But as Kushner points out, our prayers were misdirected:

> We can't pray that He make our lives free of problems; this won't happen, and it is probably just as well. We can't ask Him to make us and those we love immune to disease, because He can't do that. We can't ask Him to weave a magic spell around us so that bad things will only happen to other people, and never to us.

People who pray for miracles usually don't get miracles, any more than children who pray for bicycles, good grades, or boyfriends get them as a result of praying. But people who pray for courage, for strength to bear the unbearable, for the grace to remember what they have left instead of what they have lost, very often find their prayers answered. They discover that they have more strength, more courage than they ever knew themselves to have. [25]

Next, let us approach this issue of life's fairness from a psychological rather than theological perspective. The neurotic person frequently imagines the world to be the way he wants it to be rather than face reality as it is (this is just another aspect of resisting rather than accepting reality). He not only disregards and discounts evidence that he chooses not to see, he distorts reality to fit what he prefers or finds more comforting. We have already discussed the human tendency to seek absolute security and safety in a world where absolute security and safety doesn't exist. Other examples include this insistence that life be fair; the insistence that life be easy (Chapter Six); and the denial of death, the aging process, and our physical vulnerability (Chapter Eleven). [26]

Let me present three hypothetical situations and ask how you would react to each:

Situation #1
You've worked for the same company for 10 years and feel ready to advance into a management position. You let your boss, the owner of the company, know about your hopes in this regard. He tells you he's been happy with your work and has been planning on

offering you the night supervisor position when John retires from that job in two years. You shake hands on that understanding and over the next couple of years you do even more and better work. But when John retires in 2 years as planned, the owner gives that position to Bill who has worked with the company only 2 years (Bill by the way plays golf with the owner every weekend).

Situation #2
Your parents die within a year of each other, both in their early eighties. During their last years you drove them to their medical appointments and helped them in various ways so they could continue living in their home rather than go into assisted living — something your 2 brothers and 1 sister couldn't do because they lived out of the area. Your parents, being of modest means, left $60,000 in their will — $20,000 each to your 2 brothers and 1 sister, and nothing to you.

Situation #3
Christmas is coming and you aren't going to have much money for gifts this year for your wife and kids. The lottery is up to 30 million dollars and on an impulse you buy a couple of tickets; you know the odds of winning are astronomical but you have as good a chance of winning as anyone. Well, when the drawing takes place, not only do you not win the 30 million dollars; you don't win anything.

If the first two situations happened to you, you likely would react with anger. Over time you might even find yourself depressed. In the first situation, you might be tempted to work less hard or to start looking for another job. In the second situation, you might find yourself inclined to be less interested in holiday get-togethers with your brothers and sister. You might find yourself feeling bitter or cynical about life in general. But it doesn't take a degree in psychology to realize that a person who reacts to the third situation with anger, depression, or cynicism would be screwed up. In the first two situations, you would have been treated unfairly; something you were promised or entitled to or had every right to expect would have been denied you and given to someone else. When that happens it's common to feel angry, depressed, or even cynical or bitter. But in the third situation, even though you lost out on more money by not winning the 30 million dollar jackpot than was involved in the first two situations, you weren't treated unfairly or deprived of anything that was rightfully yours.

People expect life to be fair; they believe being a good person should protect them from calamities or even undesired outcomes. They often feel angry, depressed, bitter, cynical, self-pity or the like because they believe they have been treated unfairly or deprived of something they were promised or entitled to. But who ever promised life would or should be fair? Can you show that to me in writing or tell me who made such a promise and when? The truth is life isn't fair and no one ever promised it would be. People take what they would like to be and not only come to believe that it is; but even insist that it be so and pout, throw temper tantrums, become severely depressed, and display a wide range of neurotic emotions and behaviors when it isn't.

Let's look at clients I have seen and the neuroticism

and unfortunate consequences in their life resulting from this cognitive distortion that life should be fair. Mary, a woman in her sixties, had a dysfunctional background, had less than a high school education, was inadequate and low functioning, and was married to an unsupportive alcoholic husband. For years she had been tormented by her belief that God had punished her for an abortion she had early in life by letting her grown son die suddenly and unexpectedly of a heart attack. With her strong tendency toward guilt and self-blame, it never registered with Mary that there might be something illogical about viewing God as someone who would cause her son's death to punish her. Mary added to the unavoidable pain of her son's death a pain that was totally unnecessary— the pain of believing that she was responsible for her son's death.

I have seen a family quit going to church out of anger after the death of a 3-year-old son in a house fire. But if there was ever a time they needed religion and the support of their religious community it was then. Instead they anguished alone and isolated, and became more bitter and depressed over the years. All therapists see clients who simmer with anger and rage or wallow in self-pity because life hasn't treated them fairly. Any difficulty becomes ten times harder when we consider it unfair.

A few days ago Judy and Roy, a couple in their early sixties, came to see me for marital therapy. They reported they had been arguing since their 24-year-old son was killed in an automobile accident 13 years ago. Throughout this first session, Judy berated Roy and attacked him mercilessly for looking at other women, for wishing he could be involved with someone else, for not paying attention to her. Roy stated he did things for his wife to show he cared but these efforts were never acknowledged. They had no sexual relationship. Roy's impotency problem responded to the use of Viagra; but Judy refused sexual relations under those conditions—"If he loved me and found me attractive, he wouldn't need Viagra." Judy had no interests or hobbies, no friends, no goals or zest for life—despite having 4 surviving daughters and numerous grandchildren. She was clearly depressed and angry, even though she denied both. Any attempts to point out her destructive behavior only met with defensive and angry comments not to blame her—Roy was the cause of their problems.

I'm not sure what I will do with this couple (marital therapy with a different therapist 4 years ago was obviously of little benefit). Judy is blatantly psychologically unhealthy. (Who knows what problems her husband adds.) Her self-esteem is poor. She has little insight and little ability to look at her own behavior. She is rigid—life has to be the way she wants it to be: a husband who never looks at other women, where Viagra isn't necessary if you love someone. Notes from the previous therapist indicated this woman had never gotten over the pain and disappointment of her father refusing to pay for her to go to college—despite doing so for her two brothers. She is unwilling to let go of her anger and depression, to entertain the possibility that life could be okay despite the death of her only son, despite not being able to go to college, despite whatever other disappointments have occurred in her life.

Regarding this issue of life's unfairness, non-religious people distort reality as often and in similar fashion as religious people; the problem isn't religion but innate human fear. People find it too unnerving and anxiety producing to face and accept the obvious—life is not totally safe; awful things can happen to them and to their loved ones regardless of whether or not they behave morally. This neurotic need to distort reality in this regard, to view life as fair, is so strong that it persists despite the vast array of evidence to the contrary, despite a half dozen best selling books, both religious and psychological, pointing out its fallacy.

The belief that life is fair seems comforting; but, like all distorted beliefs, it causes more problems than it solves. The two most prevalent and destructive results of this faulty belief are anger and depression. People who externalize their frustrations react with indignation and anger. When we are treated unfairly, when we don't get what we are entitled to, we react with anger. How dare life treat me this way when I have done nothing to deserve that? People who internalize their frustrations react with depression. Tragic events that happen to them confirm what they have long suspected—they are bad and deserve to be punished (after all, bad things only happen to bad people). For such people, this belief creates guilt when there is no basis for guilt. This guilt leads inevitably to depression. Most anger and much depression stem from this seemingly comforting belief that life is, and must be, fair.

And finally, some consoling thoughts—despite life's unfairness and lack of safety:

• Suffering may not be distributed evenly, but it is distributed widely. Suffering is very private and maybe no one can share your pain, but everyone shares the reality of suffering.

• Life isn't fair but that doesn't mean we are hopeless victims who might as well just give up. Yes, there are terrible things that happen to people which make it impossible for them to live fully: children dying of cancer, diseases such as multiple sclerosis, spinal cord and head injuries. But this is the exception rather than the rule; for the majority of us life doesn't contain such overwhelming difficulty.

• We may not be able to control what we suffer, but we have a lot to say about what the suffering does to us. Some people become bitter and angry; others become more compassionate and sensitive.

• Contrary to the ineffectiveness and self-defeating nature of depression and anger in this regard, there are ways of responding and dealing with life that make it more fair, more to our liking (see Chapter Eight).

Giving up the need for a cosmic insurance package as protection from life's calamities allows for more genuine life energy. Psychologically healthy people are turned on by challenge and difficulty rather than overwhelmed with fear or denial. They enjoy the challenge of life and find creative solutions and approaches to dealing with the problems life brings. You can do the same. Accept and face life as it is. You can't control what happens to you, but you can control how you respond to what happens. More important than what happens to you is how you deal with what happens because that determines your character and the degree of self-respect and true peace and satisfaction in your life. You don't need life to be fair. You don't need life to be fair, period. Life may not be the way you would like it to be, but it is a totally undeserved gift of great value. Accept it unconditionally, embrace it wholeheartedly, live it with intensity and commitment.

Before concluding this chapter with a quotation from Albert Ellis, Ph. D. let me create the setting. I saw Dr. Ellis give several presentations and therapy demonstrations when I was in graduate school 35 years ago. In the recent summer of 2000, I had the pleasure of seeing him again in that situation—this time giving a workshop for several hundred mental health professionals, but now at age 86. The workshop was energetic, entertaining, and informative. He concludes his best selling book:

Let unfortunate things happen. Let people and things plague me. Let me grow older and be more afflicted with physical ills and pain. Let me suffer real losses and sorrows. Whatever may be, I am still largely the creator and ruler of my emotional destiny. My head and body may be bloodied, but I am still determined to be unbowed. In spite of life's storms, I shall seek and find some decent shelter. But even when I occasionally don't, I shall refuse to throw up my hands and whine and whimper. My goals are to live and let live. This is the only life I am sure I will ever have. I am delighted to be alive. I am determined to stay alive and find some kinds of happiness. No matter what, no matter what! This is the greatest challenge I can take. I fully and enthusiastically accept it! [27]

23 — *Your Erroneous Zones,* by Wayne W. Dyer (New York: Avon Books, 1977), p. 173. Reprinted by permission of HarperCollins Publishers Inc.

24 — *When Bad Things Happen to Good People,* by Harold Kushner (New York: Schocken Books, 1981).

25 — *When Bad Things Happen to Good People,* by Harold Kushner (New York: Schocken Books, 1981), p. 168.

26 — Another label for neurotic distortion of reality is "denial." The person directly denies the reality he doesn't want to acknowledge; or, when that is not possible, he ignores that reality by blocking it out of his conscious awareness.

27 — *A Guide to Rational Living,* Third Edition, by Albert Ellis and Robert Harper (Hollywood: Melvin Powers Wilshire Book Company, 1997), p. 252.

Chapter SIX
DON'T EXPECT LIFE TO BE EASY

There was once a hard-working and generous farmer who had several idle and greedy sons. On his deathbed he told them that they would find his treasure if they were to dig in a certain field. As soon as the old man was dead, the sons hurried to the fields, which they dug up from one end to another, and with increasing desperation and concentration when they did not find the gold in the place indicated.

But they found no gold at all. Realizing that in his generosity their father must have given his gold away during his lifetime, they abandoned the search. Finally, it occurred to them that, since the land had been prepared, they might as well now sow a crop. They planted wheat, which produced an abundant yield. They sold this crop and prospered that year.

After the harvest was in, the sons thought again about the bare possibility that they might have missed the buried gold, so they again dug up their fields, with the same result.

After several years they became accustomed to labor, and to the cycle of the seasons, something which they had not understood before. Now they understood the reason for their father's method of training them, and they became honest and contented farmers. Ultimately they found themselves possessed of sufficient wealth no longer to wonder about the hidden hoard.

Thus it is with the teaching of the understanding of human destiny and the meaning of life. The teacher, faced with impatience, confusion and covetousness on the part of the students, must direct them to an activity which is known by him to be constructive and beneficial to them, but whose true function and aim is often hidden from them by their own rawness.

Sufi Parable of the Greedy Sons [28]

I'm thankful for having grown up on a farm. Farmers have a strong work ethic; they are not afraid of hard work. There are daily chores that need to be done day after day after day (milking the cows, feeding the pigs); there is seasonal work that has to be done when the time demands (harvesting the oats, planting the corn). Farmers don't waste time paying attention to whether they feel like doing these chores. They do them whether they feel like it or not. They do them when they're healthy and when they're sick. They do them in nice weather and when it's freezing cold or unbearably hot. They don't expect life to be easy.

Kevin came for therapy because he forced himself to throw up (purge) 4 to 5 times a week; he knew this behavior wasn't normal and that it was both physically and psychologically unhealthy. His symptoms were consistent with bulimia except he didn't binge eat (eating an incredibly excessive amount of food in an out of control frenzy), and the personality dynamics underlying his behavior weren't consistent with those for bulimics (where self-concept is extremely poor and the person attempts to compensate by being reasonably thin and therefore physically attractive). Kevin, age 37, was 5'8" and weighed 165 pounds. He was divorced and a devoted father to his son (he had custody); he had good values and good character. He was basically a nice guy and reasonably healthy psychologically; his self-esteem was fine. But Kevin had one glaring personality flaw, and that flaw negatively impacted, and had always impacted, several important areas of his life—he disliked and avoided hard work. In elementary school and high school he did just enough to get by. In college he did the same; he got his Bachelor's Degree but never came close to applying himself to the full extent of his ability. He had his own computer business and made a comfortable living, but regretfully acknowledged that he could and should have been more successful than he was. He wanted to remarry but he put little energy into looking for a suitable partner. Regarding the eating disorder behavior, he wanted to stay thin to be attractive to women. He didn't like to diet and go without; he enjoyed sports but wasn't willing to workout. Purging was simply the easiest way to accomplish his desired goal of staying thin, and he had a long history of taking the easy way.

I diagnosed Kevin as having an eating disorder—that diagnosis fit his eating behavior; but no diagnosis described the personality traits underlying his eating disorder as well as his behavior in several other areas of life. Psychology has no diagnostic category for the lack of will power, the inability to apply oneself to anything approaching the full extent of one's ability—even when this flaw becomes extreme and interferes significantly with one's life. My therapy with Kevin focused on his eating disorder behavior, and his business practices and dating efforts, as resulting from his tendency to take the easy way. Kevin benefited significantly when he learned not to be afraid of hard work.

Being willing and able to apply oneself regardless of difficulty, to persevere at any and all cost is one of the most valuable and necessary qualities for living effectively. You can find ways to survive without it, but you can't achieve much of significance in life without hard work. Dan Millman comments:

> *If your purpose in life is to make life easier, don't get married, don't have children, avoid responsibilities, work minimally for basic subsistence needs, and learn to live cheaply. Don't commit and never volunteer. Don't own things, because they break. Hitchhike through life. Rely on the goodwill, charity, or tolerance*

of others. If you run out of family or friends to help, there's always the government. [29]

Many people in our society lack this ability to apply themselves regardless of difficulty; they see work as distasteful and beneath them. Many students don't study; many workers don't work. People pretend that marriage is easy and then blame their partner when it isn't. People take antidepressants while refusing to do anything to change personality factors or life circumstances accounting for their depression. They abuse drugs and alcohol, they don't exercise, they watch frivolous movies and TV shows, they refuse to read anything of substance. Too many people want life to be easy and insist on being entertained along the way.

People who become successful aren't that much smarter or more talented than their less successful counterparts; they are decidedly more willing to work and able to apply themselves whenever necessary (they have strength of will). People who end up being doctors, dentists, lawyers, teachers are people who select these goals and then work hard persistently to reach them. They are focused on completing the task, attaining the goal, regardless of whether it is easy or difficult. They don't quit when things get hard. They do well no matter how they feel. They aren't afraid of difficulty; they set specific challenging goals and then systematically proceed to do whatever needs to be done to achieve those goals.

The cognitive distortion that life should be easy leads to the belief that you have to feel like doing something before you can do it. The healthy mature person does what needs to be done regardless of feelings. He gets the job done even when the motivation isn't there. Many people let their feelings control their behavior; they use their feelings as an excuse for behavioral irresponsibility: "I just didn't feel like getting up," "I didn't feel like doing my homework," "I couldn't get motivated." Such people do fine as long as they are motivated and enjoy the task at hand; the problem is what they don't do when they don't feel motivated and don't enjoy the task at hand. Healthy people are able to do what they choose and want to do even on days when they don't feel motivated. That's will power, strength of will, character. Being that kind of person brings immense satisfaction and confidence in one's ability to deal effectively with life.

In my thirties, I ran 5K's (3.1 mile races). When that became not very challenging, I moved up to 10K's. In my forties I ran half-marathons (13.1 miles) and then marathons (26.2 miles). In my fifties I became bored after 15 or 20 marathons because they were relatively unchallenging—I was never better than a middle of the pack runner but I always finished. I started doing distances longer than marathons (ultra marathons). I did fifteen 50-mile runs before trying my first 100-mile run. When that 100-mile run in Ohio went well (with a 30-hour time limit, I finished in just over 28 hours), I started training for Western States, a 100-mile run in the Sierra Nevada Mountains in California (a tougher run than the 100-mile run in Ohio). That run starts at Squaw Valley and immediately climbs straight uphill for the first 4 miles. The mountains are brutal. I dropped out at 48 miles, missing the cutoff time. Just as well, given I had bad blisters and severe calf cramping and was utterly exhausted.

My goal of successfully completing Western States was put on hold for nearly 3 years following a bad automobile accident (see Chapter Eleven). But I remain determined, even moving to Sacramento to be able to train on the mountainous Western States course. Attaining this goal is made more difficult by the fact that participation depends upon being selected in a lottery process (the field of 800 entrants is roughly double the run's capacity), and by the fact that I will be in my early to mid sixties.

I'm not the only one intrigued with such challenges. Every fall a thousand runners do the JFK 50-mile run outside Washington D. C. (originally part of President Kennedy's National Fitness Program). There is even an Ultra Running Magazine because the demand is there. More and more people pay large entry fees to participate in ultra-endurance events of all types, such as the Eco-Challenge. They do this because it's a way of testing the human spirit. These events often are located in places like Death Valley or the Sahara Desert. They have names like Mountain Masochist or Quivering Quads. The tougher and more demanding the environment and conditions the better.

These events are symbolic of life in general. It's important to not be afraid of difficult, demanding things; how can you manage life if you can't manage yourself? Successful people keep going whether they feel like it or not. They train, they prepare, they motivate themselves. But in the end they have the strength of character to continue on if at all possible. Sometimes they succeed through sheer will power. They aren't afraid of difficulty, pain, failure. They are determined to be tougher than life, and the tougher life is the better. And if they fail, at least they tried.

Procrastination is a strange behavior (or lack of behavior). I didn't know much about procrastination on the farm. I first encountered procrastination in graduate school—a friend completed her doctoral course work but never finished her dissertation (and hence never received her degree). I see a great deal of procrastination in clients, as well as in friends and acquaintances—people who want to make the sales calls, want to lose weight, want to go back to school; but never do. They plan, motivate themselves, break the task down into manageable steps; they do everything they can to make the task easy enough so they are likely to complete it. They miss the point entirely. Their resolve should be to enjoy the difficulty, enjoy the challenge. If it was easy, everyone and anyone could and would do it.

I don't believe in breaking things down into manageable steps or in rewarding oneself for each step taken. These are efforts to convince oneself that the task is not that difficult. But successful people get turned on by difficulty; just tell them something is impossible and see their response. The first runner who completed the Western States 100-mile run referred to earlier, Gordy Ainsleigh, did it when it was a horse race. His horse broke down before the start, and he accomplished the task on foot, something nobody thought possible. Difficulty develops inner strength, resolve of character, strength of will, absolute determination.

How does one develop the ability to do something that is personally difficult even when one doesn't feel like doing it? Dan Millman comments with tongue in cheek:

1. You can direct your energy and attention toward trying to fix your mind, find your focus, affirm your power, free your emotions, and visualize positive outcomes so that you can finally develop the confidence to display the courage to

discover the determination to make the commitment to feel sufficiently motivated to do what it is you need to do.

2. Or you can just do it. [30]

Some people lack strength of will in most areas of life. Other people have excellent will power in some areas but not in others—someone may have excellent work habits and exercise habits but lack the ability to control his use of alcohol or his eating habits. The following ideas should help for overcoming procrastination:

1. Strive to develop strength of will in general. Start taking action to develop the habit of loving challenge for the sake of challenge. Challenge yourself with some of the various opportunities that present themselves in everyday life. Do one of the 5-mile walks for some charitable cause. Start participating in some kind of endurance activity, at whatever level appropriate for you. Volunteer for extra work or projects. Work through the night on some project that needs to be done rather than go to sleep just because you're tired. Go one day without eating—not because that's the way to lose weight but because that's one small step toward developing will power. Learn a second language or build a deck for your house rather than hiring someone. Will power in general is a habit; if you have will power in general, that may make it easier to exercise will power in specific areas as needed.

2. Quit trying to make it easy. Clients in therapy commonly want me to perform miracles in this regard. They want magically to wake up tomorrow and suddenly be able to control their eating or suddenly be able to make those sales calls. It doesn't work that way. Start by acknowledging the complexity of change, the complexity of the specific change you want to accomplish. Can you wake up tomorrow and suddenly be able to behave differently? No, that change can be accomplished but it will take time and it will take effort. Consider the Parable of the Greedy Sons at the beginning of this chapter—it was only after several years that they became accustomed to labor and the cycle of the seasons. This reminds me of the following joke:

   A man had his hand badly damaged in an accident. He asks the doctor scheduled to do surgery, "Will I be able to play the piano after the surgery?" The doctor responds, "Yes, this surgery is standard and the chances are excellent you will be able to play the piano." "Well that's great" the man responds, "I couldn't before the accident."

3. Specify the behavior that needs to be developed or changed, and develop a detailed realistic action plan to accomplish that goal. Once the specific behavioral change and strategy have been clarified, determine what time period will be needed to achieve that goal. Acknowledge that it

will take 3 months, 6 months, 2 years—whatever is realistic given the change needed and your current life circumstances. Then make a commitment to yourself regarding the effort and the time period required. It may be helpful to concentrate on executing that action plan for shorter time periods—one day, one week, one month at a time.

4. Instead of trying to eliminate an undesirable habit or behavior, strive to develop the corresponding valuable habit or behavior. Whenever possible change the issue from a behavior to prevent or avoid (like not over-eating) to a behavior to develop and put into practice (like buying and preparing sensible portions or eating more slowly). It's easier to carry out certain behaviors than it is to prevent or avoid other behaviors. This is one of the reasons why exercise helps with weight loss; it works better to go for a 5-mile run than it does to try not to eat potato chips while watching television.

5. With regards to a behavior you're trying to eliminate, make it more painful than pleasurable. Keep your cigarettes in a locked cabinet in the basement and go through the required effort for each and every cigarette you smoke; smoke standing in the cold outdoors rather than sitting in your favorite chair in the living room. Why not make it difficult and painful to smoke rather than convenient and easy?

6. Look for circumstances, organizations, and

people to facilitate and support the desired change. This is one of the reasons for the effectiveness of Alcoholics Anonymous. The person starts going to several meetings every week and actively participating, starts reading from the Alcoholics Anonymous Book every day, starts asking his higher power daily to help him get through that day and then thanks his higher power for that help each night, starts interacting and socializing with people who don't use alcohol. He surrounds himself with people, circumstances, and a philosophy of life that promote not drinking.

It takes about 6 months to develop a firm solid habit and about a year to develop strength of will in general. Waiting to do something until you feel motivated is a bad habit. Develop the habit of never wasting time trying to do something—just do it. Be persistent. If something takes a week, it takes a week. If it takes 5 years, it takes 5 years. Quit looking for the easy way, the easy task. Take on real challenges and persist until you see them through to successful completion. Develop the habit of will power and a confidence that you can and will do whatever life demands; develop the strength of will to do what needs to be done regardless. My running partner and I once went over a year without missing a 7 a.m. Wednesday morning run—despite the cold, rainy Cleveland weather. You may not be able to control your emotions; you need to be able to control what you do. In the process you make yourself a better person, someone with will power and character.

It's commonly recognized that hardship and adversity is an opportunity to develop character. Less commonly recognized is the fact that adversity and difficulty is also an opportunity to better understand one's characterological makeup (one's personality). The Eco-Challenge, one of the most extreme and demanding of ultra-endurance events, serves as an example. Teams of four spend 7 to 10 days and nights racing across the most rugged terrain imaginable, with little sleep or creature comforts, with navigational difficulties that frequently result in getting lost and having to backtrack. Participants discover in themselves and display bickering, helplessness, grandiosity, and other primitive emotions seldom experienced or displayed in less challenging conditions. After the event, participants frequently comment on the immense wealth of self-knowledge gained. While none of us like adversity, when it occurs (as it inevitably does), we might as well learn as much about ourselves as possible.

In addition to hard work, you need a direction to channel your efforts. You need goals, dreams, something that means something to you. Once I decided to write this book, I did it in about 4 years—despite working full time and having a personal life. It became a crusade; once I started the project I wasn't going to stop or be waylaid. Some people never achieve because they never decide what to do with their life. Healthy people have a career, they have relationships and children, they have interests and hobbies, they have beliefs they would die (and live) for. They are always learning new things or improving old endeavors or abilities. They don't waste time because time and life are precious. They aren't afraid of failure. Carlyle wrote that "Every noble work seems at first impossible." John D. Rockefeller said, "Whether a person expects to be a success or a failure, he's probably right." Ultimately you, rather than fate or luck, are likely to determine your degree of success in life. Sometimes life is tough; you can be tougher— or at least give it your best shot.

Life isn't easy. Pretending that it is, or insisting that it should be, only makes life more difficult and less satisfying. The psychologically healthy person not only acknowledges this, he welcomes it. He assumes responsibility for his life rather than complaining that life is too difficult. He does everything he can to make life what he wants, regardless of the effort required (and then happily accepts whatever happens). He not only is impervious to the pain of hard work; he enjoys it. Paradoxically, when you accept the fact that life is unbearably difficult, it becomes surprisingly easy.

Addendum

It is precisely our ability to manage and control our behavior that allows us to feel strongly. I can feel the full force of anger if I know I won't act on it in a way I will regret later. I can feel loss and sorrow intensely if I know I will still do what needs to be done rather than let that loss and sorrow develop into neurotic depression. Fear will never be a problem as long as I do what needs to be done despite the fear. Any mother will occasionally be irritated with her children; what's important is that she have the ability to not act on that irritation (it's okay to feel like slapping your children as long as you don't act on those feelings). A married person may feel drawn toward an affair; what's important is that he have the ability to not act on those feelings if he values marital fidelity (the marriage vow isn't to never feel like having an affair but to never have an affair). Behavioral responsibility makes it safe to feel because we are able to trust our ability to exert our values, character, and strength of will at all times—regardless of how we feel.

Chapter Six Notes

28 — *Tales of the Dervishes*, by Idries Shaw (London: Octagon Press, 1982), p 144.

29 — *Everyday Enlightenment*, by Dan Millman (New York: Warner Books, 1998), p. 51.

30 — *Everyday Enlightenment*, by Dan Millman (New York: Warner Books, 1998), p. 50.

Chapter SEVEN
PREVENTING DEPRESSION

Indolence is a delightful but distressing state; we must
be doing something to be happy.
Mahatma Gandhi

Twelve to fifteen percent of American adults at
some time in their life suffer clinical
depression—over 19 million yearly. For women
the only psychiatric disorder more prevalent is anxiety;
for men only drug and alcohol abuse and anxiety
occur with greater frequency. Its prevalence combined
with its devastating consequences make depression
one of the world's leading health problems. We all
interact on a regular basis with people whose life has
been affected by the suicide of a spouse, relative, or
friend; with some of the millions of Americans taking
antidepressant medications such as Prozac, Paxil,
Zoloft, Wellbutrin, Serzone, Effexor, Remeron, or
Celexa.

Americans seem convinced that depression is
something that just happens to people, a chemical
imbalance having little to do with life events and
circumstances or with the person's life style or
personality makeup. While it may seem comforting
to view depression in this manner, and therefore as
beyond the person's control and something he is in

no way responsible for, there are two reasons to resist accepting this view. First, it doesn't fit the facts. Second, upon closer analysis this view is anything but comforting; its acceptance means there is little a person can do to prevent or overcome depression other than take antidepressant medication or pray.

My experience working with an estimated two thousand depressed clients supports the following conclusions (all contrary to popular opinion):

1. Depression almost always occurs because of life circumstances, life styles and patterns, and unhealthy personality traits— rather than being a chemical imbalance that just happens to people.

2. People without goals, interests, and meaningful relationships are significantly more susceptible to depression than their counterparts.

3. People become depressed because they stop doing things (or their life style in general never involved doing much) more than they stop doing things because they are depressed.

4. Depressed people become less depressed when they start living and doing things again, more than they start doing things again once they overcome their depression.

5. Depression is not a healthy emotion; it is a neurotic emotion manufactured by the inability to accept life as it is.

Many life circumstances lend themselves to becoming depressed; life includes many disappointing limitations and losses: the job we lose or don't get; the health problem we are born with or develop; divorce; the death of a child, spouse, or friend; the aging process; a job we can't stand; a terrible marriage; severe financial problems. A single parent, mother of three or four young children, working two jobs to make ends meet, lacking money and time for her own needs, is understandably at significant risk for depression as she struggles on over the years. People are particularly prone to depression when they feel trapped, when they see no relief or end in sight. Past life circum stances also make us susceptible to depression: childhood sexual abuse, overly critical parents, the early death of one's parents, being rejected or ridiculed as a child or adolescent by one's peer group.

It's rare that I see a depressed client without the cause or reason for his or her depression being blatantly obvious and understandable; usually it would be surprising if the person weren't depressed. The saying "Life is a bitch and then you die" is overly cynical; but even at its best, life isn't easy. To make matters worse, we all deal poorly and ineffectively with life, causing further frustration and disappointment; we make life worse than it needs to be. We refuse to face and deal with problems. We make blatantly foolish choices and decisions. We succumb to impulsivity, laziness, greed, and cowardliness. We abuse drugs and alcohol and take poor care of our health.

Facing this reality may seem discouraging, but doing so leads to great benefit. In contrast to the concept of depression as a chemical imbalance that just happens to us without cause or reason, the more we face the truth about depression the more we realize that much of our depression is caused by factors under our direct influence. Indeed, as this chapter will clarify, there are a great many things we can do to prevent or overcome depression. Depression almost always occurs because of life circumstances, life styles and patterns, and unhealthy personality traits; and those are all factors we can, at least to some extent, change.

Depression involves a state of feeling sad, empty, discouraged, hopeless, helpless, "down in the dumps." The diagnosis of Major Depression involves feeling this way most of the day nearly every day and/or a loss of interest or pleasure in most anything and everything. Other symptoms of depression include loss of appetite or over-eating; insomnia or sleeping too much; anxiety or physical agitation; slowed speech or body movements; fatigue or loss of energy; feelings of worthlessness or guilt; diminished ability to think, concentrate, make decisions; suicidal thoughts or behavior; loss of motivation; diminished sex drive; withdrawal from life and people; low self-esteem; irritability; and crying spells.

Some people are biologically more prone to depression—just as some people are biologically more prone to anxiety, panic attacks, anger, high blood pressure, or ulcers. Under stress different people are predisposed to deteriorate in certain ways. Only 15 to 20 percent of depressed clients have a genetic predisposition for depression, however; and it is only a predisposition—not an inescapable reality waiting to happen. Chemical imbalances occur in depression; and, as a result, I commonly refer depressed clients for medication. These chemical imbalances, however, usually occur as a result of, and as part of the process of being depressed (due to the lethargy and lack of physical and mental activity), rather than serve as the cause of the depression. If the depression is severe and entrenched, an antidepressant is likely to help because clinical depression, with its ever-increasing inactivity, leads to chemical imbalances that often respond well to current antidepressant medications.

Twenty years ago I rarely referred clients for antidepressants; they simply had too many disturbing side effects. I currently refer clients for antidepressants more readily because the newer antidepressants have fewer side effect problems. Don't be misled, however, into believing that these medications are virtually free of undesirable side effects. Approximately 30 percent of clients on these newer antidepressants experience sexual side effects involving orgasm problems or loss of sexual interest. Headaches, weight gain, dizziness, nervousness, tiredness, difficulty sleeping, tremor, nausea, diarrhea, and other side effects all occur with some regularity (in 2 to 10 percent of people treated). [31]

The newer antidepressants, including the SSRIs (selective serotonin reuptake inhibitors) such as Prozac, are an improvement over their predecessors only with regard to having fewer side effect problems. Their effectiveness in combating depression is about the same as for previous antidepressants. Contrary to what has been promoted in the public mind, these medications are far from a miraculous cure for depression; only 60 to 70 percent of depressed people improve to any significant degree with these medications. Some people experience remarkable improvement, some moderate improvement, some no improvement. My estimate regarding clients I have seen in psychotherapy who were prescribed these medications is that 30 to 40 percent quit taking them due to side effect problems, insignificant benefit, or both.

Depression occurs at twice the rate for females as for males. This may be due in part to hormonal factors; the few instances I see of depression without apparent cause usually involve women whose subjective judgment is along those lines. Many sociological factors exist, however, which likely account for much of this discrepancy. The fact that drug and alcohol abuse is the leading psychiatric disorder among American men undoubtedly accounts for the depression of many American women. Women often work in addition to caring for children and being homemakers, women on average get paid less than men, women more frequently are the victim of sexual abuse and domestic violence, culturally women are discouraged more from being assertive.

Unhealthy personality traits often play a major role in depression. Poor self-esteem and problems being assertive are prominent in this regard. I frequently see women in therapy who grew up in an environment where they were devalued and where their wants and needs were discounted. This often leads to co-dependency (showing more concern for the needs of others than for one's own needs) and to being dependent on the approval of others. This personality profile (poor self-esteem, unassertiveness, co-dependency, and excessively needing the approval of others) renders a person particularly susceptible to depression. Other personality traits that play a role in depression include pessimism, being too dependent, self-pity, shyness, timidity, perfectionism, indecisiveness, and over-conscientiousness.

Suzanne, age 20, came to therapy suffering Major

Depression; symptoms included suicidal thoughts and feelings, insomnia and sleeping too much, loss of appetite, fatigue, withdrawal from life and people, feelings of worthlessness and guilt, low self-esteem, irritability, and crying spells. She was in danger of losing her job as a clerk in a women's clothing store because of missing work (staying in bed most of the day). She lived with a boyfriend in an arrangement where she did most of the household tasks and paid most of the bills (she had no idea what he did with his money). He demanded her time and attention; yet did little for or with her. The relationship was going poorly and she saw that as entirely her fault.

Suzanne grew up with an alcoholic physically abusive mother and a father who moved out of state and made no effort to stay in contact with his children. With little support, guidance, or encouragement, she did poorly in school and became involved with an emotionally and physically abusive boyfriend—while working to help support the family and often being responsible for taking care of her younger sister. Her childhood did little to help her develop the skills necessary for dealing effectively with life and fostered problematic personality traits in that regard: low self-esteem, timidity, unassertiveness, excessively needing the approval of others, an acceptance of being used and abused.

Therapy over 8 months, consisting of an antidepressant and 15 therapy sessions, led to a charming, happy, sociable young woman who was dealing more effectively with life. She ended the relationship she was in, developed an active social life, and started attending the local community college part time. Suzanne had gained a belief in herself and in life. All the factors, including the personality traits that accounted for the highly depressed young woman who came for therapy had been changed for the better.

In the first therapy session, as part of the process of gathering information I regard as relevant for therapy, I inquire of the client what their interests or hobbies are, how many friends they have, whether they are involved with anyone romantically, what their immediate and long-term goals are. People without goals, interests, and meaningful relationships are significantly more susceptible to depression than their counterparts. Healthy people have a life and having a life is precisely what makes and keeps them healthy. It takes unusually devastating events to depress such people; and even then they tend to overcome their depression rather quickly. Being truly alive in life's many and varied aspects, having interests and curiosity and passion, being active and doing things, living with purpose and intensity is a strong prohibitive factor for all neurosis, including depression.

The activities and aspects of life that people become interested in are unlimited. I encourage clients not to look on any possible interests as trite or beneath them. More important than what a person's interests are is that they have interests, because having interests is what makes people alive, interesting, healthy, non-neurotic. For years I had the pleasure of playing bridge with someone who has written over a dozen books on the game. This individual was absolutely fascinated with the complexities and nuances of bridge; so much so that he was drawn to tactics and approaches outside the stream of popular thought—sometimes, if nothing else, just to see what would happen. He loved bridge so much it's hard to imagine him becoming mired in depression. If you give life a chance, there are so many fascinating opportunities that depression might never enter your mind or your life.

Jack, a client I'm currently seeing for depression, had been highly successful in his career. His profession, however, was stressful and demanding (sixty-hour weeks including weekend and evening hours were a way of life). For reasons of professional advancement, he moved every 4 to 5 years. With work being extremely demanding, it was difficult to keep starting over in all the various aspects of life. Over the years he slowly sacrificed more and more areas of his life. At some point he quit dating. Later he quit exercising. As he slowly put on weight, partly out of embarrassment he quit socializing. As his life became more and more limited in scope, he became more and more depressed. Work became the only life he had. Then he became too depressed to continue that; he resigned his job, thinking that he would switch careers—maybe becoming a cross country truck driver. Once he quit working, even though that eliminated the stress of his job, his thinking and functioning deteriorated even further; his lethargy and lack of activity became more extreme. He used the same plate over and over to avoid having to do dishes. He wore the same sweats around his condominium so as to avoid having to do laundry. To avoid having to wash the sheets, he at first slept on the couch; when his back would no longer tolerate that, he slept on a blanket on top of the sheets. He ate TV dinners rather than cook, he didn't clean his condominium, and even his personal hygiene suffered.

People become depressed because they stop doing things (or their life style in general never involved doing much) more than they stop doing things because they are depressed. Likewise, they become less depressed when they start living and doing things again, more than they start doing things again once they overcome their depression. Depression didn't just happen to Jack. He felt trapped in a job he strongly disliked because he had no other way of maintaining that level of income. He slowly lost more and more of the essential aspects for a happy life (hobbies, friends, a romantic relationship). The more he withdrew from life, the more depressed he became; the more depressed he became, the more he withdrew from life—the all-too-common downward spiral of depression.

Jack was tried on several antidepressants, with little or no benefit. With the help of therapy, through considerable determination and fortitude, Jack seems to slowly be reversing this spiral of deterioration. He recently completed trucking school and has gotten the necessary licenses and certifications for that profession. He has returned to hiking the trails in the metro parks that he frequented in his childhood and has lost weight. As he slowly recaptures more of a life, he is becoming less depressed.

A recent study at Duke University found aerobic exercise as effective as antidepressant medication in treating Major Depression. In addition, after 10 months those continuing aerobic exercise had fewer relapses than those taking the antidepressant. While some practitioners are skeptical of this study's specific conclusions, few question the significant potential benefit of aerobic exercise in regards to both the prevention and treatment of depression. Interestingly, the new antidepressants help the brain process serotonin—the same thing that occurs with exercise.

Our bodies are meant to be active; with extensive periods of being inactive (sleeping too much, sitting around all day, avoiding people and activities) our body and mind lose their natural healthy functioning. This is just another example of the "use it or lose it" phenomenon. Depression frequently leads to a frozen physical state and greatly diminished mental abilities such as concentration, memory, decision making— all of which interfere significantly with a person's ability to act and thus promote a never ending spiral of deterioration. The only thing likely to change that is a return to being active.

It's easier to prevent depression than it is to overcome depression once it has become entrenched. In the ongoing process of depression our physical systems become dysfunctional —both our body and our mind. I have seen depressed clients who previously were athletic, lose physical fluidity and flexibility; clients who previously were intelligent and intellectually active, become confused, bewildered, and intellectually slow. Insomnia and loss of appetite can leave a person sleep-deprived and deprived of adequate nourishment and nutrition. Someone who wasn't able to deal effectively with life circumstances before such mental and physical deterioration is unlikely to cope better with those circumstances in such a deteriorated state.

Roughly two-thirds of depression goes untreated (for whatever reason, people tend to ignore and deny their problems rather than deal with them). When depression is treated, commonly the person gets an antidepressant from his family physician—without seeing a psychiatrist who is better trained regarding such medications and never going for psychotherapy.

Studies consistently show, however, that psycho-therapy by itself or in combination with an anti-depressant is more effective than an antidepressant alone. Anyone suffering pronounced depression would be well advised to seek psychotherapy to look at life circumstances, lifestyles and personality traits to see what could be done in this regard to help alleviate the depression. This less than ideal reality is perpetuated by people's tendency to look for easy solutions, by cost-cutting motives in health care, and by profit motives in the pharmaceutical industry (in 1995, for example, 2.5 billion dollars was spent on Prozac alone).

With regard to psychotherapy with the depressed client, many therapists emphasize the importance of correcting the depressed client's cognitive distortions. But depressed people already are entirely too much in their head and not enough in the present living and doing; getting them out of their thoughts is more important and more effective than correcting their thinking. Getting the depressed person active requires considerable therapeutic skill since getting active is the last thing a depressed client feels like doing; but easy or not, that's precisely what needs to be accomplished. In combating your own depression, do everything possible to return to being active.

I will never forget one client of mine named Joe. Diagnosed with cancer and facing radiation treatments, Joe made an agreement with himself that he would avoid becoming depressed by actively maintaining and fostering his sense of humor. He inundated himself with humor—Laurel and Hardy movies, The Three Stooges, comic movies, joke books. I'm happy to report Joe is alive and doing well 5 years later; but even if he had died, I'm confident he would have died laughing. I've never had the courage to suggest such a "simplistic" remedy to a "seriously" depressed client—maybe I should.

What can you do if you are already depressed (in addition, if you so choose, to seeking psychotherapy and perhaps medication)? You can do a great deal, although it may not be easy. Get back to living and doing; almost any action will help. Acknowledge and attempt to change, resolve, or improve circumstances contributing to your depression. Look at your life style and patterns with regard to how complete a life you have and what you could do to improve that. Examine personality traits and areas of rigidity that affect your ability to live with satisfaction. In their order of importance, you would do well to consider the following:

1. Face the problems in your life rather than pretend they don't exist. What are the situations or circumstances in your life that frustrate you the most?
   Are you working too many hours?
   Has your marriage become anything but what a marriage should be?
   Are your children spoiled or out of control?
   Is your weight affecting your self-esteem or limiting what you are able to do?

2. How healthy is your life style? Do you have a life? Are you blocking out important aspects of life?
   Do you have interests and hobbies?
   Do you have meaningful relationships?
   Have you developed and maintained sexual vitality?

Do you have a job or career you enjoy or find interesting?
What do you do to stay intellectually alive?
Do you have goals for the next 6 months?
Do you have goals for the next 5 years?

3. What personality traits or flaws interfere with your ability to live and be happy?
    Poor self-esteem?
    Problems being assertive?
    Codependency?
    Self-pity?
    Needing the approval of others?
    Pessimism?
    Shyness?
    Perfectionism?

4. Do you have a drug/alcohol problem?

5. Are you staying physically active—getting cardiovascular exercise?

6. What are you doing to maintain and foster your sense of humor?

Life's difficulties notwithstanding, depression is not a healthy emotion; it is a neurotic emotion manufactured by the inability to accept life as it is. Sadness, sorrow, a sense of bereavement or loss are healthy painful emotions; depression is never healthy and never necessary. Psychologist Albert Ellis explains the difference between sadness and grief, which are normal and healthy, and depression, which is unnecessary and unhealthy:

"Oh, come now!" you may protest. "You don't

mean to say, Drs. Ellis and Harper, that if my mother dies, my mate leaves me, and I lose a fine job—that even then I don't need to feel seriously depressed?"

But we do mean exactly that. No matter what happens to you, with the exception of continuous pain, we do not think it necessary to make yourself horrified or depressed. But we do believe that you will find it desirable and healthy to make yourself quite disappointed, frustrated, and grieving....We distinguish between healthy feelings of sorrow or irritation when you lose something you desire; and unhealthy feelings of depression or rage stemming from your refusal to accept frustrations, and from your whining that they absolutely must not exist. If you think rationally (self-helpingly), you will feel greatly disappointed or sad about the loss of a person you care for. But you need not also feel utterly over whelmed and depressed about the same loss. [32]

Sorrow and sadness are appropriate feelings in response to the painful things that happen in life, the catastrophic losses that take place, the devastating personal problems that occur. Psychologically healthy people feel and acknowledge their pain; but they return to living and handling everyday responsibilities. Despite their pain, they do not retreat from life; they don't allow their sadness and sorrow to indefinitely drastically affect what they do. Most sorrow and sadness fades with time—unless it is constantly re-stimulated and kept intensely alive through neurotic resistance to life. Acceptance of life as it is prevents sorrow from festering and developing into depression; despite their grief, healthy people quickly recover their inner sense of peace.

Some life events, however, are so extreme as to be unacceptable to most anyone; in those instances, another type of nonresistance is necessary. Eckhart Tolle explains:

> If you cannot accept what is outside, then accept what is inside. If you cannot accept the external condition, accept the internal condition. This means: Do not resist the pain. Allow it to be there. Surrender to the grief, despair, fear, loneliness, or whatever form the suffering takes. Witness it without labeling it mentally. Embrace it. Then see how the miracle of surrender transmutes deep suffering into deep peace. [33]

I always encourage depressed clients to face and experience their pain—rather than run from it or pretend it doesn't exist (which is just another form of resisting reality). Clients fear that in doing so they will become even more depressed, but that only happens if they re-stimulate the pain through self-pity or anger over life's unfairness or difficulty. People who are willing to face and experience their depression always regain emotional peace (even if the pain never goes away). Accepting reality as it is always works better than resisting reality; the more difficult and painful reality is, the more true that is.

As difficult as life often is, there is no need to stay mired in depression. But this requires a profound degree of psychological health attained by relatively few individuals. It requires a commitment to life that many people can't begin to comprehend. Anyone can be happy when he gets what he wants; it takes a profoundly healthy person to be happy regardless, even in life's most painful conditions. But this is the only path to true happiness because life inevitably includes pain, loss, and suffering—and eventually death. This acceptance of life as it is, this ability to be happy regardless of how life treats us, is not supported in our culture where the painful and the sad are viewed as unfair and unbearable. At funerals we act and interact as if death is tragic, the worst thing that can happen in life; but if death is tragic then life is tragic—because death is part of life (see Chapter Eleven). Death is sad and painful, but it is not tragic. The only real tragedy is that many people never really live and many people live in vulgar obscene ways.

While most of us never achieve such a profound degree of psychological health, we can at least approximate it. The previous chapters provide a foundation for a life less susceptible to depression:

Chapter One: The Art of Being Unreasonably Happy
Going for the ride freely no matter what, accepting life as it is rather than resisting life is the core ingredient for avoiding all neurosis, including depression.

Chapter Two: How to Have Healthy Self-Esteem
Low self-esteem is a crucial component of depression. Being focused on living rather than oneself, realizing that the best self-concept is none at all allows one to avoid this minefield altogether.

Chapter Three: Overcoming Fear and Anxiety

If a person withdraws from life in a fearful anxious manner, he will be deprived of life's joy, satisfaction, and meaning. Anxiety and depression often occur simultaneously in the same person because depression is a natural consequence of restricting the scope and quality of life so characteristic of the fearful anxious person.

Chapter Four: Be Flexible—Be Balanced

Flexibility and balance promote one's ability to deal with life effectively, thereby greatly reducing the likelihood of depression.

Chapter Five: Don't Expect Life to be Fair

Any difficulty becomes ten times harder when we consider it unfair. Can you accept the fact that life isn't fair and let go of self-pity? Do you have the ability to accept loss and limitation and to move on with life? How solid is your commitment to overcoming adversity?

Chapter Six: Don't Expect Life to be Easy

Pretending or insisting that life be easy leads to inertia and failing to assume responsibility for one's life—leaving one susceptible to depression. In contrast, strength of will is a dynamic life energy that serves as a shield against the hopeless, helpless, lethargic depressive attitude. It both prevents the onset of depression and is crucial for overcoming depression (where one needs to act despite not feeling like it).

The ideas presented earlier in this chapter for preventing and combating depression are within most everyone's ability. The ability to be happy regardless of how life treats us, the unconditional acceptance of life as it is, requires greater psychological health—so much so that many people would view it as impractical, if not impossible. But I see clients of every economic and educational level who deal with life's trials and tribulations precisely this way. They take responsibility for themselves and recognize that it is up to them to develop whatever potentialities they have—regardless of the circumstances life presents. While their counterparts frequently experience depression in response to life's difficulties, they live with a prevailing profound sense of happiness and satisfaction.

Chapter Seven Notes

31 — See *Feeling Good —The New Mood Therapy*, Revised and Updated Version, by David Burns (New York: Avon Books, 1999). This informative book on depression includes a detailed description of the various antidepressants, including their potential side effects.

32 — *A Guide to Rational Living*, Third Edition, by Albert Ellis and Robert Harper (Hollywood: Melvin Powers Wilshire Book Company, 1997), pp. 88-89.

33 — *The Power of Now: A guide to Spiritual Enlightenment*, by Eckhart Tolle, p. 184. Used with permission from New World Library, Novato, CA, 94949. www.newworldlibrary.com

Chapter EIGHT
LETTING GO OF ANGER

Anger is a signal, and one worth listening to. Our anger may be a message that we are being hurt, that our rights are being violated, that our needs or wants are not being adequately met, or simply that something is not right. Our anger may tell us that we are not addressing an important emotional issue in our lives, or that too much of our self—our beliefs, values, desires, or ambitions—is being compromised in a relationship. Our anger may be a signal that we are doing more and giving more than we can comfortably do or give...There is, however, another side of the coin: If feeling angry signals a problem, venting anger does not solve it.

Harriet Lerner, Ph. D. [34]

In my sophomore year in high school, we had a history teacher we disliked. Among the cruel games we played with Mr. Wagner, I'm ashamed to report, was periodically to devote certain days in his class to getting him uncontrollably angry. More often than not, he obligingly fell into our trap. In a sophomoric mixture of boredom and cruel humor, we took delight in proving that we could control his behavior; that we were in control of his class, not him. We somehow felt we won when we made him a raging maniac. Our behavior certainly didn't say anything positive about us (hopefully we've all matured since those days); but the events indeed made Mr. Wagner pathetic—an adult credentialed teacher being jerked around by idiotic sophomores with nothing better to do for entertainment.

Your life in many ways will be like being the teacher in Mr. Wagner's class; hopefully you will fare better than he did. Periodically you will be confronted with craziness, immaturity, unfairness, and great disappointment. Such behavior and circumstances will emanate from immature adolescents, lousy drivers, lazy and incompetent coworkers; but it also will emanate from your government officials, your closest friends, your parents, your children, your spouse—and from life itself. You can respond with anger if you want; but what will that accomplish other than raise your blood pressure, destroy your happiness and tranquility, and make you look like an idiot? Acting on anger is ineffective; it seldom solves the problem. Anger elicits anger, resentment, retaliation, resistance, passive-aggressive sabotage, avoidance. Anger only gets what you want as long as you have the ability to intimidate and punish the target of your anger. Few individuals are so inept and so helpless as to remain indefinitely victimized by someone's bullying anger.

Winners don't get angry; losers get angry—losers of athletic contests, losers of lovers, losers of jobs. Chronically angry people tend to be losers period, losers at life. I was Head of Psychological Services in 1995 at a men's maximum-security prison in Portage, Wisconsin. I left that job after 6 months because most of the inmates were destroyed by anger and consumed with hatred to the point of no return. The prison was full of men who thought they were bad enough to bully their way through life—but there are always more restraints, more locked gates; always someone tougher. Most inmates lacked flexibility; they continued to respond to life in the same self-defeating, ineffective ways over and over—despite the never-ending negative consequences. They seemed incapable of change, of adaptation, of learning new skills; they automatically and predictably responded to most life circumstances in their angry, confrontive, violence-threatening ways. Most inmates seemed destined, almost determined, to remain losers in the arena of life. Their pervasive anger routinely resulted in negative outcomes; the negative outcomes in turn preserved and even intensified their anger.

Angry people have limited coping skills: poor self-esteem, poor impulse control, poor judgment. They know little about the best self-concept being none at all; their self-concept is so fragile that they feel compelled to defend it at every turn. With their exaggerated need to prove and defend their manliness, they feel less of a man to walk away or avoid craziness—so they spend life confronting and reacting to every form of craziness that enters their life. With poor self-control and poor judgment, they are prone to use and abuse alcohol and drugs which only intensifies their impulsivity and poor judgment. Angry individuals commonly act-out in self-destructive, indiscrete ways in various areas of life—sexually, legally, occupationally, and regarding their own health and self-preservation. As their indiscretion grows, so does their tendency toward violence.

Acting on anger is a crude, unenlightened, unsophisticated, barbaric coping mechanism that is almost always inappropriate and ineffective in the civilized world. People who act on anger lack the ability to discover more effective ways for dealing with life. Angry people are slow learners, some of the least flexible people on the face of the planet. Compulsively angry people, without a choice about how to respond, may be intimidating; they're also pathetic. Anger, like all emotions, needs to be under your control rather than you being under its control. Consider road rage. Here we have someone who has lost all ability to choose how to respond; the rage response is so automatic and so intense that it becomes absolutely predictable. There is a loss of free will with the person's behavior being determined and controlled by someone else—cut in front of him and he has no choice but to react as a maniac, lunatic, temporarily insane person. Such a person, much like Archie Bunker, is a comic caricature of humanity, getting jerked around by every idiot on the road—much like poor Mr. Wagner.

Psychologists see people for anger management—after the person is arrested for domestic violence or reprimanded and put on probation at work for becoming verbally or physically inappropriate in a dispute with a supervisor or coworker. Anger management employs specific methods to prevent the inappropriate expression of anger or acting on anger. Possible methods include:

1. Anticipate high-risk situations and rehearse the desired response.
2. Employ delaying tactics that allow you to regain self-control such as counting to ten or taking time-out.
3. Concentrate on finding a solution to the problem.
4. Stop the anger cycle early in the process before it escalates.
5. Don't allow yourself to engage in fantasies of retribution.
6. Don't allow yourself to label others, or their behavior: labels such as "stupid," "selfish,"

"thoughtless," "vindictive."

7. Use self-affirmation techniques such as "Stay cool, stay in control," "I'm better than that," "Just because he's an idiot doesn't mean I have to act similarly."

8. Find other ways to cope with stress such as the relaxation techniques, exercise, humor.

9. Ask the other person for the specific behavioral change you want and be willing to negotiate.

10. Seek support from someone who cares about you, from an anger-support group, from a therapist.

Anger management is necessary in such situations but it isn't my main interest and isn't the focus of this chapter.[35] I'm interested in something more profound and character changing; I'm less interested in managing anger and more interested in how to get angry less often and how to release anger quickly without being damaged by it. Anyone who frequently and easily gets angry is doing a disservice to himself— regardless of how well he manages that anger. Does such a person have so little regard for his own tranquility? Does he have so little confidence in his ability to make life satisfying by some other means?

Anger is a dangerous emotion, not so much for the person it is directed at, as for the person who is angry. Anger damages a person's tranquility and happiness, physical health, and character. Much of this damage occurs even when the expression of anger is suppressed. In addition anger damages one's relationships and blocks approaches that are more conducive to solving one's problems. As will be seen, anger is ineffective and self-defeating; there almost always are more effective ways to get what one wants. Life works better and we are healthier both psychologically and physically if we almost never act on anger, if we vent anger infrequently, and if we feel angry less often.

Anger destroys any sense of peace and tranquility as discussed in Chapter One. At best anger involves at least a temporary surrendering of one's happiness. But unless anger is released quickly and completely, it becomes part and parcel of one's mood, one's general state of being, one's character; now the surrender of peace and tranquility is prevailing and pervasive. The perpetrator now is an angry person in general rather than someone who currently just happens to be angry. Anger as a mood state, rather than as an emotional reaction that is felt and then released, involves the neurotic inability and unwillingness to accept reality as it is. The angry person's life becomes a constant protest that people shouldn't do what they do, that life shouldn't be the way it is, that things that happen shouldn't happen— all forms of neurotic resistance to life rather than going for the ride freely, no matter what.

Anger is detrimental to one's physical health as well. Anger, whether expressed or suppressed, is the Type A personality trait that contributes most heavily to stress and the health problems connected to stress: hypertension, coronary heart disease, immune system dysfunction, and digestive problems. Expressing anger commonly is thought to be healthy, a way of preventing these health-damaging effects of anger. Expressing anger, however, doesn't result in feeling more at peace; expressing anger only makes a person angrier and intensifies the damaging effects of anger.

Failing to express anger doesn't increase stress or lead to ulcers; it merely controls the damage already occurring.

If anger is not released, it festers and escalates into ire, rage, fury, wrath, or hatred. These emotions take on an intensity and a life of their own; they crystallize into compulsive response patterns rather than allow a freely made conscious choice for each and every situation. This state of affairs is contrary to the balance and flexibility advocated in Chapter Four; someone with such characterological intense anger is like a time bomb waiting to be set off by the next irritating event or person—he no longer is capable of responding otherwise. Anger becomes more and more destructive, and the ability to selectively act or not act on anger becomes less and less. Acting on anger becomes a habit, and habitual anger inevitably leads to becoming a vindictive, punishing, violent, hateful person. To occasionally act on anger is dangerous but only human; but inflexible chronic pervasive anger reduces one's humanity.

Anger damages relationships because it is incompatible with love, caring, trust, intimacy, any sense of partnership; the more intimate the relationship, the more destructive anger is. The person who is the target of anger feels controlled, manipulated, disrespected. He feels brutalized, even when no physical abuse occurs. The angry father experiences his children becoming alienated from him as they progress toward the independence of adolescence and early adulthood. The angry husband, whether his wife passively tolerates his anger or fights back (if she doesn't file for divorce), has a marriage characterized by distrust, fear, and animosity rather than intimacy, sharing, and emotional closeness. His relationships with friends, sports partners, coworkers are affected similarly because anger fosters anger and resentment rather than trust, closeness, bonding.

Anger attempts to force the other person to do what you want. But people don't like to be forced or controlled, so they usually find some way to escape your control or even some way to retaliate. Angry people are perceived as dangerous and problematic; people go out of their way to unite with others to thwart and exile someone who injects anger into their world. The more anger you express the more you get pushed to the side and at best tolerated or even humored. Anger doesn't get change because people will continue doing what they perceive as important for them and their needs.

Now that we have seen the dangers and ineffectiveness of anger, it's time to look at: (1) how to minimize anger in your life, (2) the proper role of anger, and (3) a more effective alternative coping mechanism. A helpful first step toward getting angry less often is to expect unfairness, immaturity, craziness, disappointing and frustrating circumstances; truthfully you should. We have already seen that life is not fair and that disappointments are to be expected along the way. None of us is so naïve as to expect people to routinely act in mature and sensible ways; it would shock me if I ever got on the freeway and saw only sane sensible drivers. Life is a wonderful opportunity, but it also contains many challenges that will test you. Rather than live in a fantasy-world expecting life and people to always be the way you want them to be (anyone could make life work under those conditions), expect life to contain unfairness, craziness, and challenging setbacks and disappointments, as in reality it does.

People don't make you angry—you make yourself angry. The driver on the freeway, for example, who follows too closely, or who drives too slow in the fast lane, or who cuts you off in an unsafe manner might seem to make you angry—but you and your thoughts make you angry. Why should everyone drive sensibly or safely or as you would like? There are lousy, unsafe drivers in every city, large or small, throughout America (people designated by some cosmic force for that specific role); the only uncertainty is how you will react. There are drivers afraid to go over 55, drivers who can't go less than 70, drivers who use driving to vent their anger, drivers with dementia and schizophrenia, drivers who just found out their spouse had an affair. Does it really make sense to expect people to drive the way you want? To get angry and upset when they don't?

Anger happens when you think you are entitled to get what you want in a situation, when you expect people and life to be sensible and fair, or even worse to be the way you want them to be. It doesn't make sense to live in Cleveland and get angry every time it rains or snows, to live in Los Angeles and get angry whenever it's smoggy. As surely as precipitation in Cleveland or smog in Los Angeles, there will be crazy drivers on the freeway; people who lie, cheat, and steal; job promotions based on favoritism rather than work performance. How much sense does it make to get angry when those things happen, let alone for that anger to linger and fester into rage? Anger results from unmet expectations—why expect life to be fair, why expect everyone to drive sensibly when we know those are unrealistic expectations? Life often is unfair, irritating, frustrating—but you choose how you react. When you insist that life be fair, that people and the world be other than they are, you set yourself up to be angry. Expect craziness and unfairness as part of life, as indeed they are, and quit feeling victimized and angry when they occur.

The second step toward getting angry less often is empathy. The first aspect of empathy involves understanding and accepting that other people's needs and problems are as real and important as your own. People's needs inevitably conflict; your needs are no more important than those of other people. The second aspect of empathy involves understanding and accepting that other people have their own perspective, their own view of reality, their own rules for living—much the same as you. They don't agree with or like your ideas in this regard any more than you agree with or like theirs. Your "shoulds," your expectations, your rules are merely your arbitrary preferences. Angry people need to understand and accept other people's point of view; they need to drop the arrogant attitude that anyone who disagrees with them is wrong or evil. These two aspects of empathy lead to being less judgmental, less annoyed, less frustrated by the actions of others. Everyone acts for what they believe to be in their best interest; other people have as much right to pursue happiness and what they want and need as you do.

When we are mistreated or when we suffer loss, we experience annoyance, irritation, and disappointment. Anger is a normal healthy emotional reaction that serves as the acknowledgement and expression, mainly to ourselves, of our sense of loss, disappointment, and hurt. As pointed out in Dr. Lerner's quotation that opened this chapter, anger is a warning signal that our needs or wants are not being met, that our rights are being violated, that something is not right. Anger alerts us that something is being overlooked, that something needs to be done, or at the very least that something negative or painful needs to be acknowledged even if nothing can be done to remedy that.

Anger alerts us that something is wrong and provides the adrenalin and energy to act; but indiscriminant action is not what anger calls for. Acting on anger is appropriate only when faced with imminent physical threat, and even then that needs to be done with precision and control. The angry boxer who abandons the most effective strategy against this particular opponent or who attacks recklessly without adequate defensive technique is more likely to punish himself than his opponent. It is not the anger that needs expressing as much as it is the pain or loss that needs to be acknowledged and addressed. Anger needs to serve as an incentive, as a starting point for addressing and solving the problem causing the anger. Healthy people are more committed to taking care of themselves and their needs than they are to expressing their anger or getting revenge. Anger should be felt and acknowledged; but anger needs to be released quickly and completely. It needs to be kept of moderate intensity, and any uncontrolled outward expression needs to be prevented—or it will be self-defeating and block what needs to be done to solve the problem.

In contrast to the ineffectiveness of anger, assertiveness employs a broad array of techniques and skills that elicit the cooperation and good will of others: teamwork, compromise, negotiation, seeking mutually satisfying solutions. Assertiveness is the most effective course of action for attaining one's wants and needs. For that reason, "assertiveness is the antidote for anger." [36] Wouldn't you rather get what you want than get angry? In turn the better job you do of satisfying your wants and needs, the less anger you will experience.

Even if you subscribe to the philosophy that "you would rather get even than angry," the best way to get even is to enjoy life, to attain the satisfaction of your wants and needs. Paradoxically, however, the surest way to accomplish the satisfaction of your wants and needs is to want and need less. Likewise, the best way to elicit the concern and care of others is to care and be concerned about them. The lack of empathy of anger is in sharp contrast to the empathy of the mature, psychologically healthy person; and empathy, care and concern for others, and needing and wanting less (combined with assertiveness) is more effective than anger and leads to greater happiness.

Anger is based on a lack of confidence in one's ability to get what one wants. Because anger is ineffective in satisfying one's wants and needs, the angry person's sense of helplessness in this regard intensifies over time. The person who avoids getting caught up in anger, however, in most situations finds some way of attaining at least some degree of what he wants. Controlling anger reflects the self-control, discipline, and maturity that allows one to explore effective solutions to one's problems; often such a person responds to frustrating situations in ways that change rather than just bemoan the unfairness. The following Sufi story about Mulla Nasrudin exemplifies this:

Nasrudin went to a Turkish bath. As he was poorly dressed the attendants treated him in a casual manner, gave him only a scrap of soap

*and an old towel. When he left, Nasrudin gave
the two men a gold coin each. He had not
complained, and they could not understand
it. Could it be, they wondered, that if he had
been better treated he would have given an
even larger tip?*

*The following week the Mulla appeared
again. This time, of course, he was looked after
like a king. After being massaged, perfumed
and treated with the utmost deference, he left
the bath, handing each attendant the smallest
possible copper coin. "This," said Nasrudin,
"is for last time. The gold coins were for this
time."* [37]

Mulla Nasrudin would have been justified on the
first visit to be angry and to leave no tip at all. But the
approach he took led to a desired and fair result, just
not in the natural balanced progression many people
would expect and demand. This dilemma occurs
frequently in life; you can act on anger over being
mistreated or you can act so as to elicit better treatment
in the future. Sensible behavior sometimes gets
rewarded later rather than immediately. Many people
commonly resort to anger or direct confrontation
rather than employing more effective and enlightened
methods for getting what they want.

There are ways of sidestepping life's hostile forces,
or even using resistance to acquire a desired outcome.
Therapy expert Milton Erickson, M. D. reported an
early childhood experience to make this point:

*My first well-remembered use of the double
bind occurred in early boyhood. One winter
day with the weather below zero, my father
led a calf out of the barn to the water trough.*

After the calf had satisfied its thirst, they turned back to the barn but at the doorway the calf stubbornly braced its feet and, despite my father's desperate pulling on the halter, he could not budge the animal. I was outside playing in the snow and, observing the impasse, began laughing heartily. My father challenged me to pull the calf into the barn. Recognizing the situation as one of unreasoning stubborn resistance on the part of the calf, I decided to let the calf have full opportunity to resist since that was what it apparently wished to do. Accordingly, I presented the calf with a double bind by seizing it by the tail and pulling it away from the barn while my father continued to pull it inward. The calf promptly chose to resist the weaker of the two forces and dragged me into the barn.[38]

Direct confrontation usually meets with resistance. There are other methods of responding that are more likely to achieve the desired outcome. Anger lacks the flexibility necessary for trying and discovering these alternative coping mechanisms.

Television's Lieutenant Columbo serves as another example of the skillful use of unorthodox methods to achieve desired outcomes. For lack of a better term, I refer to his approach as "slip sliding around." Imagine having to do Columbo's yearly evaluation—he hasn't been to the shooting range in years, dresses inappropriately, doesn't follow procedures; yet he solves cases. His approach seems to disarm, confuse, and surprisingly often produce unaccountably positive results. People seem less threatened, less guarded and defensive in dealing with this seemingly inept investigator than they would if he were the traditional authoritarian policeman. Even if he poses a serious threat to someone's best interests (if they committed the crime), it's hard to be angry with him, hard not to like him, hard not to become engaged in conversation with him.

You may fear that not getting angry will make you a pushover—that's wrong. Nothing is more forceful than the person who calmly, without emotion, in no uncertain terms lets you know that he will stand up for himself and what he wants. A calm, firm, assertive approach works better than anger and is the response of choice of healthy people. Anger reflects a loss of control and therefore a loss of effectiveness; assertiveness reflects self-control and therefore the ability to use one's resources effectively. People who get angry feel, and often are, helpless and inept in dealing with life. Assertiveness is more effective and more conducive to physical and psychological health.

Psychologically healthy people are flexible—they have a vast array of approaches and coping mechanisms for dealing with life and they choose how to respond to each and every situation rather than reacting compulsively in any set manner. They ignore or walk away from craziness and crazy people because they know there is no sensible way to respond to craziness; they are more interested in living life than in proving their manhood. They know that a positive reward system works better than anger—rewarding the desired behavior rather than punishing the undesired behavior. They can and will react with anger, but only as a last resort—in contrast to the angry person who habitually and compulsively resorts to anger in response to every problem he encounters. Psychologically healthy people are able to acknowledge, experience, and feel their anger without concern because they trust their ability to control their behavior despite feeling angry. They seldom suppress their experience of anger but they often repress their expression of anger and their acting on anger because doing so promotes better character, makes life work better, and leads to greater tranquility. But even more importantly, they have a philosophy of life that leads to feeling angry less often.

I frequently hear other therapists complain about the angry, unpleasant, abusive clients they see. I seldom experience that. I like to think, and I believe this has to do with how I deal with clients and life in general. The more you stay in the present, and accept reality as it is, the happier you will be and the less anger you will have. The less angry you are the less anger you will encounter. Eckhart Tolle states:

> I have observed that people who carry a lot of anger inside without being aware of it and without expressing it are more likely to be attacked, verbally or even physically, by other angry people, and often for no apparent reason. They have a certain emanation of anger that certain people pick up subliminally and that triggers their own latent anger. [39]

To a large extent, you determine not only your own degree of happiness but also the mood and character of the people you encounter in life. Rather than letting other people make you angry, and triggering anger in others that they then interject into your world, why not create a life characterized more by empathy, acceptance, and tranquility?

The goal is to live life rather than letting your energy get diverted into neurotic emotions and neurotic resistance to life. No human reaction or behavior is as diametrically opposed to this goal as unnecessary anger. The more you live without experiencing anger or acting on anger unless absolutely necessary, the healthier you are. Living in such a manner takes determination and practice; but it is a realistic goal that can be attained by the following:

1. Cherish your inner peace and tranquility; surrender it reluctantly.

2. Don't expect life and people to always be the way you want them to be.

3. Don't confuse what you want in life with what you need. We want many things but need very few.

4. Whenever possible, sidestep life's hostile forces.

5. Care and be concerned about others.

6. Develop the habit of consistently responding in a calm assertive manner.

7. Rather than acting on anger over how you have been treated, act so as to elicit better treatment in the future.

8. Reward the desired behavior rather than punish the undesired behavior.

34 — *The Dance of Anger*, by Harriet Lerner (New York: Harper & Row, 1985), pp. 1-4. Reprinted by permission of HarperCollins Publishers Inc.

35 — Any reader with a pronounced anger management problem is advised to read *When Anger Hurts* by Matthew McKay, Peter Rogers, and Judith McKay (Oakland: New Harbinger Publications, 1989) which deals extensively with anger management and the chronically angry person.

36 — *When Anger Hurts*, by Matthew McKay, Peter Rogers, and Judith McKay, p. 184. Copied with permission from New Harbinger Publications, Oakland, CA. www.newharbinger.com

37 — *The Pleasantries of the Incredible Mulla Nasrudin*, by Idries Shaw (London: Octagon Press, 1983), p. 24.

38 — *Varieties of double bind*, by Erickson, Milton and Ernest Rossi. The American Journal of Clinical Hypnosis, 1975, 17 (3), pp. 143-144.

39 — *The Power of Now: A Guide to Spiritual Enlightenment*, by Eckhart Tolle, p. 21. Used with permission from New World Library, Novato, CA, 94949. www.newworldlibrary.com

Chapter NINE
MAKE YOUR MARRIAGE A SUCCESS

The idea that conflict is healthy may sound like a cruel joke if you're feeling overwhelmed by the negativity in your relationship. But in a sense, a marriage lives and dies by what you might loosely call its arguments, by how well disagreements and grievances are aired. The key is how you argue—whether your style escalates tension or leads to a feeling of resolution.
John Gottman, Ph. D. [40]

Marriage is not easy. A happy marriage, with harmony and teamwork, not to mention a vibrant sexual relationship, is more the exception than the rule. Statistics regarding modern American marriage reveal an expected longevity of only 7.2 years, with 43% of marriages ending in divorce. Approximately 1.2 million divorces occur in the United States each year, breaking up families involving more than one million children; the damage and emotional pain is obvious. In addition, however, many people who stay married are miserable in their marriage—staying because of fear or for the sake of the children; the damage and emotional pain, while less immediate and obvious, is equally substantial. A third of my depressed clients wouldn't be depressed if they weren't in a painfully problematic marriage. Such marriages foster substance abuse, anxiety, anger, over-eating—virtually every form of psychological pathology. The children in such families fare no better than children whose parents divorce.

More so than any other relationship, marriage requires two psychologically relatively healthy individuals—with many of the traits and qualities advocated in this book. The psychologically unhealthy person has too great a need to be loved and/or too little ability to love. He is too insecure and too bound by compulsive strategies for dealing with life to intimately coexist with another person. Such a marriage, instead of a relationship in which both people enjoy each other and grow together, is characterized by manipulation and control—to satisfy the neurotic partner's needs. A marriage in which both partners are significantly impaired is often hopelessly problematic.

A pattern seen frequently by therapists is a self-negating, martyr, codependent woman married to a selfish, controlling, emotionally withdrawn man who is incapable of seeing his partner as an individual in her own right. The woman seeks therapy (either individual or marital) because of her unhappiness. She is in pain, and complains about that pain; but she has a deeply ingrained inability to directly assert and act for her own needs and rights. Such marriages often remain intact, despite being dysfunctional, because the man is unmotivated to end it and the woman is incapable of doing so.

The first step toward achieving a healthy happy marriage is to be a healthy happy person. To accept and love another person, and to be happy in the process, you must accept and love life and be happy in the process of living. Attaining happiness through a knight in shining armor is an adolescent fantasy, based on faulty cause and effect reasoning. Marriage is not a cure for neurotic misery; if you're miserable with life in general, don't expect marriage or your partner to make you happy. Happiness can only be attained through the struggle for psychological health. Psychological health doesn't guarantee a happy successful marriage, but such a marriage is impossible without it.

The second step toward a successful marriage is choosing a suitable partner, someone capable of dealing effectively with the difficulties involved. Choosing a mate is one of the most important decisions we make; it deserves and requires time, reflection, and good judgment. A mistake carries a heavy price: the rest of one's life trapped in misery and frustration or a messy divorce with children subjected to anywhere from less than ideal circumstances to chaos and abuse. I have seen hundreds of clients whose life has been a living hell because of the person they married—clients who were subjected to physical abuse, chronic blatant infidelity, alcoholic rages, financial disaster. And they see their children subjected to the same indignities and often turning out disastrously as a result. Yet few people make a careful, studied choice about who to marry. A discouragingly high number of people marry when they discover the woman is pregnant, so in reality a choice is never made. The marriage process resembles Russian roulette—if you're lucky the choice turns out fortunate; but often there's a bullet in the chamber. A strange phenomenon is the surprising number of people who marry even though they know it's a mistake; I have seen dozens of clients who cried tears of sadness the night before their wedding or the honeymoon night.

I'm currently seeing Barry for difficulties connected to one of the nastier divorces I have seen. After filing

148

for divorce, his wife fabricated accusations of his abusing their 2-year-old son, refused him visitation privileges as ordered by the court, and refused to pay bills and undertook a campaign of reckless spending in an attempt to ruin him financially (regardless of the consequences for her and their son). I feel badly for Barry; he is paying dearly for the poor judgment he exercised in his choice of a partner. Barry proposed a month after they met. They married 5 months later, despite numerous jealous rages on her part—including one over his rather innocent bachelor party at a racetrack. Barry understands too late that this was not a sensible way to make a decision of such importance.

There is no need for marriage to be a disaster. In this chapter I describe how to substantially increase the likelihood of having a successful marriage. I first present general issues of importance for a successful marriage; then describe traits to avoid in a potential mate, including common problem issues in a male mate and female mate respectively; then discuss what to do if unfortunately you're married to an impossible partner; and lastly describe how two suitable partners can function effectively to make their marriage successful and happy.

General Issues

Marriage, like life in general, isn't easy. Failing to recognize that only makes marriage more difficult. Be sure your expectations of marriage and your partner are realistic; unmet expectations are the primary source of misery and anger.

Just as being self-centered and self-preoccupied lends itself to being neurotic and interferes with one's ability to live effectively, enriching the life of your partner is a healthier focus than concentrating on what your partner does for you. This of course works better the healthier the partner you choose.

Marry someone you like as they are, rather than hoping they will change or that you can change them into what you want.

Sexual attraction is necessary. You can't force yourself to be romantically in love with someone; it takes chemistry. Many marriages take place where one of the partners never was physically attracted to their partner.

Take into account what kind of parent the prospective mate would make. You're subjecting not only yourself to risk, but your future children as well. In addition, someone who would be a poor parent likely will be a poor mate for the same reasons.

Marry someone not too different than you, but also not too similar. Healthy differences add richness to marriage rather than promote rigidity and boredom. Will the two of you have a harmony of similarity; yet have enough dissimilarity to add to, enrich, and complement one another?

Qualities to Avoid in a Mate

A potentially good mate will have many of the traits described in this book for psychological health; most importantly they will be balanced and flexible as discussed in Chapter Four. Be leery of someone as a potential mate who is rigid; and the more rigid they are, the more leery you should be. Life works as well as someone's biggest flaw. We all have problems, but a flaw that is out of control will make marriage impossible. Nothing, including all the marital therapy in the world, will help your marriage if you marry an idiot—someone who has a serious behavioral or personality flaw that they refuse to acknowledge or deal with even though it significantly impairs their ability to live sensibly. An "idiot" by definition refuses to change. If he/she were willing to change, he wouldn't be an idiot; he would be a person with flaws and weaknesses like everyone else. There will be chaos in such a person's life—including their marriage. In choosing a marital partner, be leery of someone with any of the following traits—presented in their order of destructiveness and danger for a successful and happy marriage:

1. Avoid jealousy and possessiveness at all cost. Jealousy has nothing to do with love; it reflects pathological insecurity. Profound insecurity is one of the most destructive and dangerous of the personality flaws and is difficult to eradicate. Insecurity somehow will always bite you in the ass.

2. Avoid over-control. Love cares about the other person, what they want and need, what is important to them. Love supports the other person and what they want to do and become rather than trying to control or change them into what you want.

3. Avoid anger. Anger is selfish and controlling; it is incompatible with love and caring. And anger tends to generate action and frequently leads to abuse.

4. Avoid substance abuse! Millions of Americans are waiting for their spouse to quit abusing alcohol or drugs; it happens, but betting your future happiness on this certainly proves that love must be blind. I have seen many clients who quit abusing substances when they had children; unfortunately, their partner never quit.

5. Avoid the person who is too selfish to love and make sacrifices for others, too self-centered to care about and support others. Such a person lacks the most essential quality for being a mate or parent. At the extreme in this regard are sociopaths, who get through life by using others. Women sometimes get conned by the sociopathic man who is charming, flattering, entertaining, bright—but dishonest, irresponsible, lazy, manipulative without guilt or remorse.

6. Avoid the person who needs too much, who expects you to make them happy, who lacks solid self-esteem.

7. Avoid the person who isn't ready to settle down (they may never be).

8. Avoid the person who can't work; who lacks discipline, responsibility, reliability.

9. Avoid the person who smothers you.

10. Avoid the person with a weak character and a weak sense of commitment and values;

the person who cares little about family, friends, the human race.

11. Avoid the person who lacks a good healthy sex drive (but also avoid the person who thinks only of sex). Sexuality can be difficult to maintain in marriage as it is, without one person lacking sexual interest from the start. The frequency of a total lack of sexual intimacy in marriages is alarmingly high.

12. Avoid the person who is unable or unwilling to be emotionally intimate.

I see clients who miss the big picture here. If their first marriage ended disastrously because their spouse lacked character and stability, for their second marriage they choose someone with excellent character and stability; but ignore some other important factor or flaw—like pronounced substance abuse. If they divorced their first husband because he was unwilling to do things and be with other people, they next marry someone who is outgoing and social but incapable of marital commitment and fidelity. Unfortunately their second marriage is as frustrating as their first, only for different reasons.

In our society there are certain ways in which both men and women respectively are prone to be out of balance. There will be exceptions (like the man who is passive and unassertive or the woman who is aggressive), but the gender specific tendencies are there and clarifying them shouldn't shock or offend anyone. In our society more women go to therapy; more men to prison. If someone is out of balance, they're likely to do so in accord with the gender specific stereotypical expectations that underlie and account for many of life's realities. Men are expected to be rugged, strong, take charge, a little wild to sow their oats. Women are expected to be loving, weaker, less sexual. The following issues are problem areas for men and women respectively:

> Men: substance abuse, anger, violence, over-control, lack of emotional intimacy, jealousy, out-of-control sexuality, being sociopathic.

> Women: low self-esteem, being needy and insecure, resentment and resulting anger, depression, codependency, problems being assertive, lack of sexual interest.

What to Do if You're Married to an Idiot

Everyone brings flaws and limitations to a marriage, but some people are impossible as a marital partner. An important issue is what to do if unfortunately you're married to an idiot. As an example, let me discuss a client named Sharon. At age 70, she came to therapy with the same issues and circumstances as when she had seen a different therapist 3 years previously. For the entire 20 years of her second marriage her husband had been an idiot: he refused all sexual contact as well as any and all physical affection; the only thing he did was watch sports on television; he refused to participate in family or social activities of any kind; he was cheap and paranoid about spending money; he did nothing to celebrate holidays, birthdays, or anniversaries; and of course he refused to go with her for marital therapy or even to talk with her about their marriage. In the first therapy session, she kept giving me more and more examples of her husband's insane behavior—long after it should have been abundantly clear to both of us that her husband was, and always had been impossible as a husband. She kept asking, "Why does he do these things; why is he the way he is?" I pointed out to her that those might be fascinating issues to explore if she wanted to become a clinical psychologist, but understanding why he was as he was or did what he did woulnd't change her marriage. Her husband did these things because he was an idiot and idiots do idiotic things. One of the things they do is refuse to change; Sharon had enough evidence to be certain her husband wasn't going to change to any significant degree.

Her previous therapist advised Sharon to leave her marriage; I pointed out that, while I had my opinion on the matter, I would not tell her what to do. Neurotic fear and financial insecurity had a lot to do with why she stayed in the marriage. She was paying a huge price for security; but it was her life and she had a right to do whatever she chose—going out into the world alone at age 70 on $600 a month social security wouldn't be easy either. What she shouldn't do, however, was stay in the marriage but continue to be upset by her husband's behavior. If she stayed in the marriage, she needed to accept (not necessarily like) the fact that he was the way he was; and to concentrate on making the best of it—doing things with her children and grandchildren and with friends, participating in activities herself despite his refusal to accompany her, living as completely and sensibly as possible despite her marital frustrations. This made sense to Sharon; she tried that approach and found herself less miserable.

If you're unfortunately married to an idiot (who by definition refuses to change), either leave the marriage or live as sensibly as possible given the circumstances. Don't stay in the marriage but continue to get angry or depressed because your partner isn't the way you wish they were. Don't demand or expect a miracle; don't insist that reality be different than it is. Those reactions will only make you neurotic in addition to your already difficult situation.

How to Make Your Marriage a Success

When couples initially come for marital therapy, commonly they immediately proceed to argue and fight, interrupt one another, attack each other's character, and proclaim an endless list of their partner's misdeeds and shortcomings—and then look to me as the referee whose role it is to decide who's right and who's wrong. They assume that marital therapy is a safe place to engage in such behavior and that somehow this is the way to go about marital therapy. I joke with these couples that if they will loan me a coin, I will decide who is right. I explain to them that as their therapist I will do everything possible to interrupt and prevent such behavior because it is incompatible with marriage and marital therapy. As a marital therapist, I'm not as interested in the content of what's being said as I am in the process between the couple—and this is not the right process.

Most couples I see in therapy attribute their problems to poor communication. While poor communication is often a factor, it virtually never is the main problem. Marital problems develop and escalate because love isn't easy. As a marriage deteriorates, love more and more gives way to anger and selfishness. The couple becomes less willing to listen to one another; they treat each other with more contempt and less respect. John Gottman, Ph. D., a professor in the Department of Psychology at the University of Washington in Seattle, has conducted years of research with hundreds of couples to determine the most important factors for a successful marriage. He summarizes his findings with the following: "I can offer two pieces of advice based on what I've observed among stable couples in my research. The first is to have realistic expectations about your marriage. The second is to treat your spouse with love and respect."[41]

Marriage demands and depends on love; nothing will make up for a lack of love. If you love someone, you care about them; you care about what they want and need; you care about where they are in life and what's important to them. Healthy couples can be assertive, they can each speak up for what they want; but because of love, they never cease to care about what their partner wants. In deteriorating marriages both people feel their partner doesn't care about them—so why should they care about their partner? But someone has to break this stalemate. The best way to get your partner's love, unless you're married to an idiot as described above, in which case nothing is likely to help, is to do everything you can to care about your partner and what they want and need. To make your marriage work, never cease to care about and love your partner.

Behavior that is acceptable in one marriage may be highly destructive in another—depending on whether the couple views that behavior as compatible or incompatible with love. Some couples interpret ranting and raving at one's spouse as an insult and a clear lack of love; other couples view such behavior as merely allowing each other to vent their frustrations and something they can do precisely because they love each other. While couples vary regarding the behaviors acceptable to them, the following principle remains valid for all couples: Avoid any behavior that you or your spouse regards as incompatible with love.

The acceptability of "fighting" in marriage is partly a matter of semantics. The process between a couple needs to be consistent with love. A certain amount of arguing is inevitable, and even healthy—as long as neither person loses touch with caring about the needs and wants of their partner. But fighting, in the literal meaning of that word, is incompatible with marriage. Fighting implies contending against and striving to defeat a rival or enemy; it implies a winner and a loser. There is no winner when couples fight, when couples try to force their will on the other person. Healthy couples express their individual desires but they always continue to care about and give respectful consideration to the desires of their partner.

More recent research by Gottman[42] indicates that most couples never resolve many of their problems and differences. Healthy couples resolve the problems they can and accept those they can't; they accept their differences and continue to enjoy the other person despite those differences. Unhealthy couples continue to try to force the other person to change to meet what they prefer, and become more bitter when and if that doesn't happen. Ironically many divorces occur after one person changes to meet what their partner insist they be; eventually their partner becomes bored with them because they have ceased to be a real person. Differences are healthy; they offer each person in the relationship a chance to develop flexibility and balance.

What is most important in a marriage is the atmosphere the couple creates, the way they treat each other in the inevitable reality of not resolving their problems and differences. As explained in the quotation opening this chapter, how couples handle conflict largely determines the success and quality of their marriage. Conflict is an opportunity to learn about your partner's wants and needs and to show that you care. Unfortunately it is an opportunity often ignored or missed as couples respond to conflict with selfishness, anger, over-control, fighting, and even verbal or physical abuse. Too many couples spend too much time trying to get the other person to change, too often in a not very loving manner.

The biblical verses read at marriage ceremonies (1 Corinthians Chapter 13) remind the couple entering into marriage that, "Love is patient and kind; love is not jealous, or conceited, or proud; love is not ill-mannered, or selfish, or irritable; love does not keep a record of wrongs." Based on such principles, the following is what love looks like; this is what I want from couples when I see them for marital therapy (both in the session with me and in the week or two between sessions). I want them to listen to each other instead of interrupting each other. I want them to encourage each other to speak up for what they want instead of trying to force their will on the other person. I want them to praise each other more and criticize and blame each other less. I want more humor and less anger, more patience and less irritability, more kindness and less indifference or cruelty. I want them to react less defensively and more out of love and concern. I want them to move toward teamwork and collaboration rather than polarizing into their individual isolated solitary positions.

The literature on marriage refers to such acts of love as "bids" or as "deposits in the bank account of marriage." Research shows that for a marriage to succeed and endure there needs to be at least 5 bids or deposits for every negative act or withdrawal. The frequency of such acts of love is more important than their magnitude; a trip to Europe is unlikely to repair a marriage with otherwise few deposits (a simple "good morning," asking how your partner's day went, holding hands, going to your partner's preferred restaurant rather than the one you prefer, a smile, making coffee, etc.). Marriages that allow more negative behaviors require more frequent positive behaviors. If ranting and raving at your spouse is acceptable in your marriage, it is still a negative behavior that needs to be offset by at least 5 positive behaviors. Unfortunately, besides the danger of too few bids being made, bids often go unnoticed or are even rejected. Filmed interactions of couples in marital therapy reveal that in poor marriages 50% of bids go unseen. Unseen bids, and even more so rejected bids, become less likely to be repeated.

Marriage needs to be based on friendship, but marriage is more difficult and demanding than friendship. You can detach yourself from a friend and come back weeks or months later. Marriage involves a complex interweave of each person's personality traits, personal preferences, and dearly held beliefs and values—often in circumstances where somebody has to make concessions in areas such as the handling of money, sexual patterns, parenting styles, household and family responsibilities, and general life styles. It's not surprising so few marriages are successful and happy; but it doesn't have to be this way—most of us don't use half the ability we have in our marriage. Challenge yourself to do better than this. Make the positive bids and be open to noticing and acknowledging those of your partner. Look over the behaviors and qualities of love described above and challenge yourself to make your behavior toward your partner consistent with that.

If I could offer only one recommendation regarding how to make your marriage a success, it would be to accept and enjoy your partner for the person they are rather than trying to control or change them. Difference is healthy; it leads to growth and flexibility. One of the greatest dangers in life is becoming too rigidly the way you are. The worst choice you could make might be to marry someone exactly like you think you need, someone too much like yourself. In addition, accepting and loving your partner as they are makes you a healthier person; the inability to do that is merely another form of neurotic resistance to life. Whenever you find yourself wanting your spouse to change, look instead at how you could change to solve the problem. Paradoxically, the more you accept your partner as they are, the more likely they are to change.

Many couples deal poorly with their differences in another way. If the man is irresponsible financially, the woman will handle their finances; but this means that the man never will develop financial responsibility. Healthy couples deal with these issues in a totally different manner. The partner who is good at a particular skill helps their partner develop that ability. They help their partner to become more social, more playful, more responsible, more assertive—rather than protecting them from dealing with those issues. As a result both partners become better balanced and thus healthier psychologically. Psychological health is invigorating and lends positive energy to a marriage that can serve many positive functions. The opposite promotes neurotic rigidity in each partner and the resulting neurotic traits are a threat to the future of the marriage.

I recently saw a couple for premarital therapy. The woman lacked assertiveness and confidence; the man was confident, forceful, and opinionated. Both individuals were likeable and relatively healthy psychologically. I pointed out to this couple that if their marriage functioned well, she would become more confident and assertive and he would become more partnership oriented. If their marriage functioned poorly, she would become less confident and assertive and he would become more controlling and domineering. There is interplay between our flaws and those of our partner. Often we are right in the change we think our partner needs to make; but we fail to recognize that it would be healthy for us, and our marriage, if we became less like what we think they need to be.

The ideas presented in this chapter don't always work—because marriage isn't easy and many of us aren't healthy enough to truly love. We approach marriage with the same unrealistic expectations and neurotic distortions that we have about life in general. But marriage, because of the difficulty involved, requires extraordinary psychological health, insight, and sophistication. Marriage is more an opportunity to give and to grow than an opportunity to get and to have life easy (difficulty is always an opportunity for growth and greater self-awareness). It requires our best effort and our most advanced skills. It helps to have an awareness of the flaws and rigidities that make it difficult for someone to coexist with us, and an awareness of the flaws and rigidities that make it difficult for us to coexist with them. Such awareness makes marriage more interesting and enjoyable and improves the prognosis for a successful and happy marriage. Without such awareness, when seemingly insurmountable problems develop, we will be at a loss to determine the real problem and what, if anything, can be done to resolve the problem. In addition, psychological insight and sophistication helps immensely in choosing a psychologically healthy mate, someone relatively free of the destructive traits discussed earlier in this chapter.

All too frequently, I see couples in marital therapy where the observations each person has regarding their mate are justified and accurate. But the couple remains stuck in dysfunction because these observations are expressed as attacks rather than as straightforward requests for the person's own needs or as loving concern for their partner. You have a great deal to do with how satisfying or unsatisfying your spouse is. You can bring out the worst in them, through attacking and blame, or you can bring out the best in them through love and caring. As accurate as your perceptions and observations may be, attack and blame will elicit defensiveness, denial, and counter-attack. But loving concern for your partner and their psychological well-being might elicit a totally different response—and lead to a relationship in which both people accept and enjoy their partner as they are, all the while encouraging and supporting each other in the struggle for psychological health.

40 — Reprinted with the permission of Simon & Schuster Adult Publishing Group, from *Why Marriages Succeed or Fail,* by John Gottman with Nan Silver, p. 173. Copyright 1994, John Gottman. All rights reserved.

41 — Reprinted with the permission of Simon & Schuster Adult Publishing Group, from *Why Marriages Succeed or Fail,* by John Gottman with Nan Silver, p. 224. Copyright 1994, John Gottman. All rights reserved.

42 — *The Seven Principles for Making Marriage Work,* by John Gottman (New York: Three Rivers Press, 1999).

Chapter TEN
UNDERSTAND YOUR PAST—THEN LET IT GO

We can chart our future clearly and wisely only when we
know the path which has led to the present.
Adlai E. Stevenson

The movie *Sophie's Choice* portrays Sophie (played by Meryl Streep) living a highly destructive life—including drug and alcohol abuse, an unsuccessful suicide attempt, and an extremely dysfunctional relationship. Eventually, through the flashback technique, we are presented with the events that led Sophie to this path of self-destruction. Sophie had been taken with her 10-year-old son and 6-year-old daughter to the Auschwitz Concentration Camp. At the entrance to the concentration camp she was forced to decide, within a matter of seconds, which of her two children would be allowed to live and which would be killed in the Auschwitz ovens—if she refused to decide, both would be killed. Having one's child killed in the concentration camps often was more than mothers were able to deal with—but having to make the choice of which of your children would die in such a manner, and watching that daughter be carried away screaming and pleading for help, understandably might be more than anyone could live with. The movie ends with Sophie and her disturbed boyfriend committing joint suicide.

Some people have suffered irreparable damage and dysfunction; I hope you are not one of that real but limited group. Some life events are more atrocious and horrific than the human spirit can bear. Be leery of complaining bitterly in that regard, however, if the circumstances don't warrant that. Like the saying "I felt bad about having no shoes until I met the man without any feet," there always are people who have had it worse. Besides, if you take this victim stance, you're giving up on life and on yourself. Believing that your life has been ruined because of past events in some ways may seem comforting (and may be hard to refute); unfortunately there's nowhere you can go from there except a life characterized by anger, depression, shame, or self-pity. While many life events are highly unfortunate, few are absolutely overwhelmingly devastating. In many ways what happened to you in the past may not be as important as what you told yourself, and tell yourself now, about what happened. There are victims of childhood sexual abuse, for example, who proceed to live highly satisfying productive lives.

In my outpatient practice treating adults who generally are employed and living lives their neighbors and friends would view as normal and of the everyday garden variety, I see approximately 30 women a year, and 5 or 6 men, who report being sexually abused as children. When Kinsey's survey of sexual behavior in America reported in 1953 that 12% of females reported sexual contact when they were preadolescent girls by an adult male, the findings were considered scandalous and overstated. But studies conducted since indicate Kinsey's study under-reported the frequency of childhood sexual abuse. At least 20% of American women and 5 to 10% of American men experienced sexual abuse as children, with the most frequent age for victims being between 7 and 13. Childhood sexual abuse occurs as frequently in Caucasian and upper class families as in ethnic and lower class families.

There are more than one million confirmed cases of child abuse and neglect in America each year. I see clients who report extreme physical abuse as children: being tied up and beaten, having teeth knocked out, suffering injuries requiring medical treatment and even hospitalization. I see other clients where mental and emotional abuse was extreme: a constant barrage of being called fat and ugly, stupid or dumb, a slut or whore; a child being treated vastly worse than his siblings; a father deliberately and senselessly killing the child's dog. I see other clients where neglect as a child was equally extreme: a child kept isolated from human contact, parents preventing the child from going to school, a parent never attempting to see their child again after divorce.

People subjected to traumatic life events or blatant abuse or neglect are at risk as they attempt to live sensibly and effectively. As portrayed in the movie *Sophie's Choice*, particularly devastating events are likely to cause damage regardless of when they occur. We are more susceptible, however, to events and circumstances early in life—because of character and ego resources being less well developed. Children subjected to such factors sometimes feel unloved, unworthy, and inadequate. Going into adulthood they may lack the confidence and ego resources necessary to function effectively. Rather than developing into a strong, emotionally independent person some of these individuals develop and exhibit many of the symptoms of Borderline Personality Disorder: [43]

Low self-esteem
Depression
Suicidal behavior
Drug and alcohol abuse
Inappropriate intense anger or difficulty controlling anger
Lack of healthy assertiveness
Difficulty being alone
Over sensitivity to real or imagined rejection
Chronic feelings of emptiness
Brief turbulent love affairs
Eating disorders
Self-mutilating behavior such as cutting on themselves

If your past included severe dysfunction, you might do well to seek professional therapeutic help. If you do, hopefully that therapy will contain far less sympathy than constructive help for living effectively. As a therapist, and hopefully as a human being, I'm not callous about the suffering and abuse people are subjected to; but little therapeutic benefit, and much therapeutic harm, results from sympathy. Regardless of how dysfunctional your past may have been, I implore you to never adopt a hopeless, helpless, despairing, victimized attitude. Doing that is simply unfair to yourself and naively dismissive of your true resources and potential.

Few of our lives contain the degree of trauma portrayed in *Sophie's Choice*. Likewise, while sexual abuse, physical abuse, emotional abuse, and neglect occur with some frequency, none of these forms of dysfunction occur for the majority of us. There are many types of less severe dysfunction, however, that affect all of us—even if to a lesser extent than the more severe forms discussed above. Dysfunction refers to life events or circumstances that are likely to impair our ability to deal with life in an effective and satisfying manner.

It would be surprising if our childhood didn't involve factors that make it difficult for us to live a happy healthy adult life—either destructive things that happened or necessary things that didn't happen. No parents are perfect. All of us as children had our own problems that influenced how we experienced our childhood. Life itself contains factors that are far from ideal—parents who die with young children, illnesses that take a child out of the normal socialization circles, poverty that limits opportunities and is often experienced as embarrassing and degrading.

Humans need many factors for growth into psychological health. They need warmth and support to develop inner security and confidence. They need healthy friction with others to develop strength and their separate identity. Karen Horney comments on the factors that negatively impact psychological development:

> But through a variety of adverse influences, a child may not be permitted to grow according to his individual needs and possibilities. Such unfavorable conditions are too manifold to list here. But, when summarized, they all boil down to the fact that the people in the environment are too wrapped up in their own neuroses to be able to love the child, or even to conceive of him as the particular individual he is; their attitudes toward him are determined by their own neurotic needs and responses. In simple words, they may be dominating,

overprotective, intimidating, irritable, overexacting, overindulgent, erratic, partial to other siblings, hypocritical, indifferent, etc. It is never a matter of just a single factor, but always the whole constellation that exerts the untoward influence on a child's growth. [44]

Neurosis too often gets passed from generation to generation. Children growing up in dysfunctional families, besides failing to learn healthy family and parenting skills are prone to psychological impairment. Both factors contribute to a new generation of dysfunctional parenting—that can take any of the following forms: [45]

Not Being Taught Essential Skills
There are basic skills and knowledge that are important to live effectively. Often parents provide the basics of food and shelter but don't take responsibility for fostering the following basic life skills:

1. Sexuality
Even for people with sex education, sexuality is one of the most problematic areas for people as they try to live effectively. Without adequate sex education, the person starts at a distinct disadvantage in an already difficult area of life.

2. Intimacy
Being comfortable and knowledgeable about hugging, physical affection, emotional closeness is an important skill for living a complete life. Some families suppress and inhibit such expression, making it difficult for the person to function in these areas after leaving his/her

family of origin.

3. How to Work, Study, and Be Disciplined
It's a shame when children don't learn self-control and discipline. Many children are never helped to develop work and study habits, instead becoming lazy and directionless. Often they get lost in the web of drugs and alcohol—trying to make life one big party.

4. Socialization
Children need to learn to socialize with their peer group, to participate in the activities appropriate for their age. They need to learn to socialize with the opposite sex, including dating skills; it's helpful if they know how to dance.

Being Controlled and Dominated
Children need the freedom to explore and assert their individuality. Without that, they have difficulty knowing and asserting who they are. Too often parents raise a child in a manner too influenced by who they want or think the child should be, or to be the person one parent wishes they themselves had become.

Lack of Unconditional Love
Parents need to love their children uncon-ditionally—regardless of academic or athletic ability, personality traits, whether or not they share the parents' values or religious beliefs. Often parents favor one child over another—boys over girls, good students over poor. One of the obligations parents have to any child

they bring into this world is unconditional love and acceptance.

Pronounced Criticism

I see clients who were affected by constant parental criticism, especially from an overly critical father. They commonly end up with low self-esteem and problems with assertiveness—heavy burdens to carry into adult life.

Being Overprotected

Children need to be prepared to handle the world by early adulthood; parents who overprotect their children, despite their good intentions, do their children a disservice.

Being Spoiled

The world doesn't center on us. Parents who center the family world on the wants and desires of their child develop an expectation in that child that is inconsistent with the real world and therefore dysfunctional.

Neglect

Children require time, energy, resources; it's neglect when parents don't provide that. Parents on drugs or alcohol commonly get caught up with their own pleasure-seeking behavior and neglect their children's needs. Single working mothers often are caught in this regard in an impossible situation—there aren't enough time and resources for everyone. Parents who have more children than they can take care of and provide for do their children an injustice.

Lack of Sufficient Support

A bad combination is high expectations but little support and knowledge on how to realize those expectations. An example is parents who expect their children to get excellent grades, yet do nothing to help with homework or study habits.

Parental Personality Flaws

Parents with pronounced personality flaws and shortcomings like perfectionism, an attitude of cynicism and skepticism, or anger and temper problems increase the likelihood that their children will take on those same learned habits or will be affected negatively in some other way. For example, children subjected to angry and violent parents, especially when that is directed toward them, tend to be fearful, anxious, and timid; or to be violent and angry themselves.

Parental Faulty Ideas about Life

Parents with faulty beliefs about life pass on those faulty, unworkable, and therefore dysfunctional beliefs—like the belief that other people's approval is extremely important, almost essential.

Many people tend to view their childhood as normal, regardless of how dysfunctional and abnormal it may have been. In some instances this involves brainwashing—with the victim having been coerced to view the abnormal behavior when it occurred as normal. A couple of years ago I saw a woman in therapy (she was 80 pounds overweight, had terrible self-esteem, had difficulty being assertive, and presented with Major Depression) whose father, who was a minister, for years sexually molested her and her two sisters. She idolized her deceased father and minimized his deviant behavior—I'm sure her father presented his behavior as normal, and insisted she view it that way, when she was a child. In other instances it's more a straightforward honest perception; if your father frequently gets drunk and verbally abusive, after a while that becomes normal and expected. And yet in other instances it is a defense mechanism; we prefer to think of ourselves, and our background, as normal and psychologically healthy rather than as unusual or defective. We tend to deny our problems and pretend they don't exist.

The idea isn't to blame your past or your parents, or to avoid taking responsibility for your life. But for many individuals, it's important to avoid unnecessary self-blame as well; many individuals with problems did well to survive their childhood without even more severe problems. Usually it fits the facts better, and leads to better results, to accept and understand your past as dysfunctional but normal, and then to take responsibility for becoming healthier.

It's important to understand your past and the effect your past has on you at this time. It's good to understand the strengths you have because of your past; but it's even more crucial to understand your flaws and weak points connected to that past. Our childhoods were all dysfunctional to some extent. To become a healthier, well-balanced person requires taking steps to correct and make up for the flaws and defects resulting from your past. Professional therapy might be helpful but generally is not essential. Honesty in acknowledging these factors, and courage and determination to take corrective action, will do you fine.

Understanding the effect your past has on you at this time is complex. As quoted earlier from Karen Horney, "It is never a matter of just a single factor, but always the whole constellation that exerts the untoward influence on a child's growth." In addition, each of us plays a dynamic role in our self-development. Two children can grow up in the same environment and family and end up drastically different (as with myself and my twin brother). In reaction to controlling parents, for instance, one child may opt to react with rebellion and defiance while his sibling resorts to a compliant and submissive strategy. How these two children then continue to develop is likely to become even more diverse.

Many people refuse, usually out of fear, to take an honest look at themselves and their behavior resulting from their past. Few people examine their persona lity—their strategy for dealing with life. They routinely respond to life in rigid predetermined ways without being aware of having a choice, without noticing that other people respond differently. They lack the courage to honestly assess where they stand in life and to take responsibility for what needs to be done about that at this time. Understanding your flaws and areas of weakness, as well as your personality structure, is only the first step in the healing process; but if you have the courage to take this first step, you're likely to make yourself a psychologically healthier person.

Let me discuss my childhood as an example of what is important about understanding one's past and then taking corrective steps to become a healthier better-balanced person. My childhood was typical— considerable dysfunction of a mundane everyday variety; I wouldn't expect anyone to break out in tears of overwhelming grief or sympathy in reading this.

My childhood provided me with several valuable positive qualities. These qualities have always been strengths of mine; at every turn in life they have served me well.

1. A Strong Work Ethic
My grandparents emigrated from Germany and performed heroic toil and labor to turn forests into tillable fields, to dig roads out of hillsides (on the farm in Wisconsin we called them "sidehills") with picks and shovels. My parents went through the Great Depression. They knew the value of work and the need to survive. I learned to work as a routine part of life; I appreciate this gift highly.

2. Sound Values
My parents provided an absolutely solid sense of right and wrong, of the value and importance of life and living life well.

3. Interests and Hobbies—Enjoying Life
We went fishing 4 to 5 times a week, we played cards every night, we were ardent fans of the Milwaukee Braves and the Green Bay Packers. (In contrast, I'm concerned when a client has no interests or hobbies, no awareness of the importance of enjoying life.)

There were corresponding flaws in my childhood; I present them in their order of impact and importance in my life:

1. Being Controlled and Dominated

My mother was 35 when she had twin boys; at that stage in life, she didn't have the energy required for such a task. My parents meant well, but they didn't foster individuality and self-expression. I ended up with good values, but didn't value myself enough. I had problems being assertive; I was too perfectionistic, too compliant, too out of touch with my real self.

2. Exaggerated Drive for Success

My parents placed too much importance on being successful, being better than other people, proving oneself and getting recognition (a dysfunctional faulty idea about what's important in life). My father, who was intelligent but who had to drop out of school after the eighth grade to work on the farm, always advised, "Don't be a farmer like me." I took him seriously. I was going to be a doctor of something, I was going to get to the top even if I had to climb over others or beat their brains in.

3. Lack of Unconditional Love

There was little unconditional love. My mother was fanatically Catholic. My oldest brother was headed toward the priesthood and my two sisters (who of course couldn't be priests) and my twin brother and I were devalued in comparison—it was like competing against God for my parents' love and approval.

4. Lack of Social Skills

My social skills, especially with girls, were poor. I went to a one-room country grade school where my twin brother and I were the only ones in our grade—there were only 14 kids in all eight grades when we graduated. I then went to an all boys Jesuit college preparatory high school. I never learned to dance, never went on a date. I was painfully shy—speech class was torture.

5. Lack of Sex Education & Emotional Intimacy. I received no sex education. My parents never hugged, kissed, or showed any physical affection toward each other or toward us kids.

6. High Expectations—Little Guidance
There were high expectations but little knowledge or guidance on how to meet those expectations. My parents knew little about life in the big city, going to college, the business world. My parents only knew farming in a small isolated area. Dubuque, Iowa and La Crosse, Wisconsin, both cities of sixty thousand people, were sixty miles away; we traveled to each of them once during my childhood.

The strategy I developed for life was to be successful, but in a saintly manner—to be not only better than others, but perfect. I was overly responsible and self-sacrificing; my identity was overly connected to being useful. I placed little importance on being happy, on enjoying life; I was out of touch with emotion, passion, sexuality, intensity, and uniqueness. I was determined to accomplish and be what my parents valued rather than to discover and develop my real self—being totally unaware of the difference.

As I set out into adulthood, my first step was to enter a Jesuit Catholic seminary. I never had any interest in religion; I just wanted to be successful (and saintly) and in my family nothing compared in importance with being a priest. Being as driven and determined as I was, I stayed in the seminary 10 years. The Jesuits valued education so I had my Bachelor's Degree and Master's Degree and had taught high school mathematics for 2 years before I dropped out. But this path did little to develop my skills or comfortableness with women, sexuality, intimacy, or emotional closeness.

I next went to graduate school in psychology. In contrast to religion which never interested me, and mathematics which I was good at but had little passion for, I love my work as a psychologist. Over the course of 30 years working with clients, I gradually applied what I learned to my own life. Around the age of 50, I started to realize and deal with the insanity of centering life on prestige, being perfect, proving oneself better than everyone else. I started to become part of the human race. In the words of Hermann Hesse, "He now felt as if these ordinary people were his brothers." [46]

In my early thirties I entered into a relationship that eventually led to marriage; it ended 20 years later in divorce—almost entirely my fault. Kathy was a wonderful, kind woman; unfortunately I knew too little about love, intimacy, and self-sacrifice. It was too late to help my first marriage, but later I put a tremendous amount of time and energy into getting better in these areas. I joined dating services, placed ads in the personals, answered personals, and dated many different women—mostly unsuccessful endeavors but learning experiences (however painful). Fortunately this area of life only requires one outcome of the right person at the right time. I met my current wife Norma five years ago; she matches up well with many of my areas of weakness. I understand better now that marriage is more an opportunity to give and to grow than to have life easy. This time I think it's going to work.

While once it was torture to give a 5-minute talk in speech class, I now give presentations to large groups. I've discovered I'm a very social person in my own way. I've become more physically affectionate—I actually hug people and sometimes kiss women in greeting. Despite 30 years as a psychologist, I still have difficulty being assertive and excessively needing other people's approval—but not nearly to the extent as earlier in life. Making these changes required a willingness to work at them over time—despite fear and anxiety. Expanding one's boundaries, overcoming the limitations from one's past, however, doesn't have to be all work and anxiety; at some stage it becomes fun and invigorating.

As important as it is to understand your past and the effect it has in your life at this time, it's even more important to let go of your past. You can't avoid being neurotic without doing so. Resistance to life's past trials and tribulations always involves non-acceptance of life in general. It takes away your tranquility and effectiveness because hanging on to the past prevents being anchored in the present. Giving up the belief that past events and people have ruined your life allows you to discover how to be okay—in the present. If you can't accept the past, at least accept your pain in that regard. Quit resisting what has been and what is.

For ideas on how to let go of your past (rather than festering in anger, resentment, self-pity, guilt, or depression) review the chapters The Art of Being Unreasonably Happy, Don't Expect Life to be Fair, and Don't Expect Life to be Easy. Quit telling your story of victimization to others or to yourself. Challenge yourself to be a better parent than your parents were to you; that will be rewarding and reassuring that the damage you suffered has already been partly or even largely remedied. Accept that life is what it is and that you and your parents did the best they could. Eckhart Tolle comments:

> If you are one of the many people who have an issue with their parents, if you still harbor resentment about something they did or did not do, then you still believe that they had a choice—that they could have acted differently. It always looks as if people had a choice, but that is an illusion.... The moment you realize this, there can be no more resentment. How can you resent someone's illness? The only appropriate response is compassion. [47]

Your parents did what they did because of events in their past. If feasible, talk with them about that—in a calm assertive manner rather than as a helpless victim whose life has been ruined. Talk with your siblings or other people who grew up in similar circumstances to get ideas about how to live effectively despite your past. Realize that you might even have certain strengths precisely because of the events you so dislike. If you could somehow change your past, you wouldn't be who you are. If you develop peaceful acceptance of yourself now, you will have no difficulty accepting your past.

Maybe you weren't responsible for what happened to you in the past, but you are responsible for what you do about that now. Understanding your past is important only to the extent that it helps you take responsibility for yourself now. I believe that understanding your past, while not crucial, can be very helpful for understanding yourself now; but not everyone agrees. Eckhart Tolle suggests that concentrating on the past may be more counter-productive than helpful:

> Attention is essential, but not to the past as past. Give attention to the present; give attention to your behavior, to your reactions, moods, thoughts, emotions, fears, and desires as they occur in the present. There's the past in you. If you can be present enough to watch all those things, not critically or analytically but nonjudgmentally, then you are dealing with the past and dissolving it through the power of your presence. You cannot find yourself by going into the past. You find yourself by coming into the present. [48]

Accept responsibility for steadfastly making your life more functional and satisfying. Understand yourself (using whatever methods you find helpful)—your strategy for living and your patterns of resisting life rather than remaining committed to present moment reality; then accept the rewarding challenge of learning to live rather than remaining stuck in neurotic resistance to life. Life is therapeutic; if you're open and receptive to growth, healing opportunities arise with regularity. Not only take advantage of the opportunities that come along in life to correct your neurotic tendencies, actively seek out those opportunities. Avoid the common tendency to let fear and anxiety, or self-pity, keep you imprisoned in the limitations resulting from your childhood dysfunction. The more responsibility you take for yourself and your life now the more invigorating and satisfying life will be—and the easier it will be to accept and let go of your past.

Chapter Ten Notes

43 — In the psychoanalytic concept of that term

44 — *Neurosis and Human Growth: The Struggle toward Self-Realization*, by Karen Horney (New York: W. W. Norton & Company, 1950), p. 18.

45 — In addition to helping you understand your past and its effects in your current life, this list can serve as a guideline of problems to avoid in parenting your children.

46 — By Hermann Hesse, from *Siddhartha*, p. 106. Reprinted by permission of New Directions Publishing Corp.

47 — *The Power of Now: A Guide to Spiritual Enlightenment*, by Eckhart Tolle, p. 190. Used with permission from New World Library, Novato, CA 94949. www.newworldlibrary.com

48 — *The Power of Now: A Guide to Spiritual Enlightenment*, by Eckhart Tolle, p. 75. Used with permission from New World Library, Novato, CA 94949. www.newworldlibrary.com

Chapter ELEVEN
DEATH—THE FINAL CHAPTER

Those who have the strength and the love to sit with a dying patient in the silence that goes beyond words will know that this moment is neither frightening nor painful, but a peaceful cessation of the functioning of the body. Watching a peaceful death of a human being reminds us of a falling star; one of the million lights in a vast sky that flares up for a brief moment only to disappear into the endless night forever. To be a therapist to a dying patient makes us aware of the uniqueness of each individual in this vast sea of humanity. It makes us aware of our finiteness, our limited lifespan. Few of us live beyond our three score and ten years and yet in that brief time most of us create and live a unique biography and weave ourselves into the fabric of human history.
Elizabeth Kubler-Ross, M. D. [49]

You and I are going to die. We don't like to acknowledge and face that fact; we tend to keep that reality out of our conscious awareness, somewhere in the hidden recesses of our subconscious. When we do talk and think about death, we do so in abstract terms that deny death's impact as a real life experience. We are all aware, however, of our gradual downhill slide from youth toward old age. We see the development of wrinkles and our hair turning gray, we notice our diminishing physical strength and abilities, we maybe even notice our diminishing mental abilities—all reminders that our dying will not be an abstraction. Not only will we cease to be; we will die. For each of us, you and I included, death will be a real life experience that will take place in some specific way at some specific time. Despite all the factors that shield us from death's reality, despite our euphemisms, despite our efforts to keep the reality of death out of conscious awareness, we remain painfully aware of this real event waiting to happen. For every human being, the fear of death is as real and inevitable as death itself.

Our life progresses inevitably either toward psychological health and maturity or toward neurosis. The more neurotic we become, the more death becomes an insult to our self-concept and a source of overwhelming fear. Death forces us to grapple with the reality of being mortal like everyone else, of being dispensable. Our awareness that death awaits us at some real time and place is potentially our greatest fear; and fear, more than any other factor, is the core of neurosis. The awareness of our death provides the foundation for our tendency to be more afraid of life than committed to living fully, behind our tendency to distort reality into what we would prefer, what would make us more comfortable.

Our awareness of death doesn't have to lead to overwhelming fear. We can deal with our fear of death the same way we deal with any and all fear. We can face this fear, readily acknowledging our mortality rather than letting that awareness lurk in the recesses of our subconscious mind. We can face the reality of death and respond "So what." What exactly is it we're so afraid of? Is death and growing old really that unacceptable? Psychologically healthy people, while not liking the fact they will die, accept that reality and move on with living while they have the opportunity. Having a healthy acceptance of death leads to more peace in our life, more ability to achieve and live fully. Acceptance of death diminishes fear and allows us to live in the present with peace, tranquility, and happiness. In contrast neurotic people frequently have a great deal of anticipatory anxiety regarding death; that's what occurs with hypo-chondriacs—their life becomes dominated by neurotic anticipatory fear, all in their mind, that they have some life threatening illness.

The more someone accepts death the better that person is likely to do with life; similarly the more someone accepts and embraces life the better he/she is likely to do with death. You might think the more someone loves life the more he would hate death and the more someone hates life the more he would accept death. It tends to be exactly the opposite. Death is part of life, a life experience much like other life experiences. People deal with death as well or as poorly as they dealt with life in general. Death can be a peaceful, meaningful, termination-of-life experience or it can be an experience dominated by fear, depression, anger, denial; it can be lived in a healthy or neurotic manner depending on the psychological health of the person involved. As with life in general, we can die peacefully or in an emotionally neurotic manner.

Psychologically healthy people, with their ability to live intensely in the present, go through the process of dying with that same here and now tranquility. David Reynolds, in describing the dying process of Japanese psychiatrist Dr. Morita, reveals how, for the psychologically healthy person, death is just another life experience to be lived as intensely in the present and as purposefully as any other:

Dying is neither good nor bad. It is just part of life driving: purposeful, destination-bound driving. All the while noticing the scenery. Professor Morita, dying in Japan, asked his students to watch the medical procedures performed on him. The students were struck with his effort to use even his last breaths to teach about being a human physician. But to Morita the teaching was natural, proper, what needed to be done, the only thing to do in that moment. [50]

The same factors that make a person's life healthy rather than neurotic account for his ability to die in an equally healthy manner. Healthy people accept loss during life without depression or anger; they accept the loss of life in a similar manner. Their ability to accept life's unfairness serves them well at the time of death—what is more unfair about life than death? People who are self-preoccupied and self-centered do poorly with death. Healthy people die with the comfort of knowing that they have contributed to life and that their contribution lives on; their healthy self-esteem based upon no self-concept at all allows them to grow old gracefully and to accept the fact that life is bigger than any one of us. Even in the process of dying you can be the creator and ruler of your emotional destiny. Death is inevitable, but you determine how you react to, and are affected by, that reality. Resistance to life and death produces neurotic emotionality. Going for the ride freely, no matter what, allows you to maintain happiness even in the experience of death; happiness attains you when you surrender everything. If you find life meaningful, purposeful, acceptable, you will find death equally so. Just as surely as fear of death is the cornerstone of neurosis, peaceful acceptance of death is the cornerstone of psychological health.

Death is not as tragic as the fact that many people never really live; it is not as tragic as the loss of life to neurotic fear and the unwillingness to accept life as it is—because death is inevitable, but life being dominated and curtailed by neurosis is not. Death should make us aware of the importance of life; it should promote a craving to live intensely and sensibly. The finiteness of life makes every day important. If it weren't for death, there would be little urgency to do something today, this week, this month, this year, this decade—we could always do it tomorrow, next week, next month, next year, next decade. The finite time we have in life makes it important to use time well; that is what makes it tragic when we waste years (whether out of fear, depression, anger, lack of will power) by not making decisions and facing and dealing with life effectively. Richard Carlson, Ph. D. suggests imagining yourself at your own funeral as a method of reminding yourself of what's important in life. He comments, "It's a good idea to consider your own death and, in the process, your life. Doing so will remind you of the kind of person you want to be and the priorities that are most important to you."[51]

Freud postulated that people have a death instinct—a compelling subconscious need to hurt themselves and eventually lead to their own demise and death. As strange as this conclusion might seem, Freud felt much human behavior could not be accounted for by any other explanation. Freud's conclusion was overly simplistic. Everyone is born with a life instinct—an innate desire to live in a meaningful and satisfying manner, a desire to make life work. In the process of living, however, some people, slowly overwhelmed by life's difficulties, become more and more neurotic. Psychologically healthy people accept death, perhaps reluctantly, but they cherish life intensely, every possible moment of life. Their behavior reflects their craving for life, their well-preserved life instinct. Neurotic people, with their fear of life and their inability to accept life as it is, engage in more and more behavior that reflects their fear, anger, depression, denial, self-pity. Such behavior is often self-defeating and self-destructive; the life instinct has been damaged.

Suicide is the ninth leading cause of death in the United States (in the middle compared to other countries); yearly 31,000 Americans commit suicide. In addition, many suicides don't get reported as suicides—the driver who crashes into a tree or cement barrier at 3 a.m., the woman who "accidentally" takes too much Valium combined with too much alcohol. And for every completed death by suicide there are an estimated 25 suicide attempts that fail—over 750,000 suicide attempts every year. And as any therapist could verify, there are many more people who have suicidal thoughts and feelings than there are who act on those thoughts and feelings.

The dictionary defines suicide as, "the act or an instance of taking one's own life voluntarily and intentionally." This definition needs rethinking. Some of the things that fit this definition don't seem suicidal; some of the things that don't fit the definition seem suicidal. Were the Japanese Kamikaze pilots in World War II really committing suicide? While not part of the formal definition, suicide suggests the wasting of one's life without purpose. These pilots believed firmly that they were acting nobly and with purpose. Many parents would, and have, sacrificed their life to protect the life of their child—this seems natural and healthy rather than suicidal. A person with terminal cancer who kills himself isn't so much choosing to die as he is choosing how to die. On the other hand, every year thousands of adolescents throw their life away in high-speed, death-defying automobile accidents. (Fourteen percent of adolescents who die commit suicide, 11 percent are victims of homicide, 31 percent die in motor vehicle accidents.) Think of their marriages never formed, their children never conceived, their careers and lives never lived because of such tragedies. As blameless as anyone involved might be (good parents, conscientious teachers, caring religious leaders, decent adolescents), there was blatant disregard for life.

The last thing I want to advocate is a neurotic, fearful, cautious approach to life. But such blatant disregard for life, as if the loss of life is trivial—and all with no purpose or value to be gained. Some risk is sensible—few racecar drivers get killed, few planes crash, few mountain climbers fall to their death; and most of these activities have some benefit or value. But adolescents playing chicken at a railroad crossing? Men playing Russian roulette because they have little regard for life or an exaggerated need to be macho? While such senseless acts may not fit the dictionary definition of suicide in that the person does not wish to kill himself, in fact these people voluntarily and intentionally engage in activities that risk life without purpose or benefit. These are the acts of intoxicated, immature, neurotic, careless, or just plain stupid people. The outcomes are every bit as tragic as the thousands of completed suicides in America each and every year.

Some suicides occur because life can be extremely difficult; these difficulties understandably sometimes overwhelm even psychologically healthy people. Much suicidal behavior, however, reflects the same dysfunctional, self-destructive traits and behavior that characterized the person's life in general. Suicide often is impulsive, something the person wouldn't do if he/she took more time to think about it. This type of suicide commonly occurs in a person with a life-long deeply ingrained tendency toward impulsivity—with behavior routinely being controlled by emotions rather than the other way around. Other suicidal behavior is driven by passive-aggressive anger. In divorce, for instance, the person not wanting the divorce may up the stakes for the person filing for divorce by saying, "You can leave me but you'll have to live with the reality that I killed myself as a result." The person's suicidal behavior is driven more by attempts to punish the ex-partner than by what's best for the person himself. Again these people commonly lived lives permeated with passive-aggressive ways of responding to frustrating situations. Still other suicidal behavior is driven by feelings of hopelessness and helplessness. Frequently these people felt hopeless and helpless in dealing with difficulties throughout the course of their life. People commonly persist, at any and all cost, with their deeply ingrained ways of dealing with life— right to the end, even to the final act of committing suicide.

Suicide is no more tragic than the way some people live. It would have been less tragic if Adolf Hitler had committed suicide as an adolescent than what he did with life. How tragic is the suicide of a 75-year-old widowed man who is confined to a nursing home and almost totally helpless after a series of devastating strokes? Yet when such an individual quits eating because he chooses to no longer live, we force feed him intravenously. There are many situations where we allow, and even insist, that people suffer through what I wouldn't dream of letting my dog endure. It's ironical that our society so abhors the idea of suicide regardless of how pathetic and hopeless the circumstances—when there is no possibility of the person being able to live in any meaningful way. And yet we think little of all the ways in which people waste and throw away their life in all the various forms of insane disrespect for life.

As a society we have too much abhorrence of death and not enough regard for life. We are death phobic and foster the illusion that we will live forever. Seventy percent of medical expenses involve the last 6 months of life—often when there is little purpose. We are too obsessed with resisting death and too unconcerned about living with purpose and dignity. Death is not as sad as the fact that many people never take advantage of the gift of life.

People's refusal to take adequate care of their health is another factor supporting Freud's conclusion that human beings have a death instinct. Everyone knows the basic health habits; yet the majority of people refuse to consistently put them into practice. It is far from uncommon for people to die 10 or more years earlier than would have been necessary and for people to lose quality of life during their later years due to poor health that could have been prevented. Millions of Americans suffer debilitating symptoms from diabetes; many of these cases of diabetes could be avoided, or at least controlled, by sensible eating habits and exercise. Check with a life insurance company to see the extra premiums for those who smoke, or consider the prevalence of lung cancer for smokers compared to nonsmokers. Yet 50 million Americans continue to smoke. Any person over 40 should be concerned about the risk of heart disease and either early death or later years limited by cardiac problems; yet millions of men and women in this age group are overweight, have terrible eating habits, smoke, abuse alcohol, and don't exercise. I see adolescent clients who have screwed up a hand for life by punching a door or wall because they were angry. I see obese clients who can't fit into the chair in my office—let alone dance or walk around the block. You can only go as far in life as your body will take you. It makes no sense not to take care of your health and body; it's a slow form of suicide.

Psychological suicide, the killing of the spirit, is as catastrophic as and more prevalent than physical suicide. I began writing this chapter on a fishing boat headed south on the Sea of Cortez (the Mexican Baja). The boat of 27 fishermen, when we arrived at our destination, would split off into 3-person "pangas," each with its own guide. The success of your trip can have a great deal to do with the guide you get (determined by the hint of an unusually large tip, who one knows, one's degree of assertiveness, or in some instances a lottery system). Three years ago we managed by some combination of the above methods to get Eduardo as our guide; Eduardo was without exception regarded as the best of the best. Our trip was a smashing success, including one morning catching 9 grouper between 50 and 90 pounds each. We happily gave Eduardo an unusually large tip, partly with the expectation that doing so would increase our chances of getting him as our guide in future years. For weeks before this year's fishing trip, and during my flight to Southern California and our drive to San Felipe, Mexico, I fantasized about the chances of our getting Eduardo as our guide again this year. But an unexpected thing happened. The night before the boat departed, we ran into Eduardo in one of the local San Felipe bars. Eduardo had become alcoholic, he had lost his job as a guide, and frankly he looked awful. Well, needless to say, we didn't have Eduardo as our guide this year—sad for us but somehow the tragedy goes deeper. How sad that the best of the best wasn't any longer doing his special thing. Another killing of one's destiny, of the blessings someone had to offer all of us fantasizing "the great catch."

As I've returned to working on this chapter months later, the eastside suburbs of Cleveland where I live have been jolted this past week with one of those bizarre events that truly disturb the human soul. A woman so desperately wanted a baby that she kidnapped a pregnant woman, fatally shot her, and then performed a crude Caesarean Section and claimed the baby as her own. She then buried the real mother's body under the floor of her garage. When the police were closing in and returned to question her, she fatally shot herself. This woman met her husband when she was in prison and he was a corrections officer at that facility (hardly the ideal way to start a relationship). After their marriage, she had at least one miscarriage and was informed she likely would never be able to have a child. This woman then proceeded to fake being pregnant for the next 7 or 8 months; her neighbors, family, and apparently even her husband were taken in by her deception. She planned her atrocity months in advance. She met the victim when they both were shopping at the local Wal-Mart for baby clothes and accessories. How tragic was this woman's suicide compared to the tragedy of what she did when alive?

Life doesn't just happen to us; we have a significant impact on how satisfying or unsatisfying life is. In the process of living we become psychologically healthier or more neurotic. The healthier we become the easier life is; the more neurotic we become the more impossible life becomes. Death is our final act in life. It reflects who we have become over the course of our life. It seals and stamps into history either the love and courage with which we lived or our fear and inability to accept and deal effectively with life. Freud was partly right; some people do have a death instinct—the life instinct has been badly damaged. But life doesn't have to be as difficult as many people make it. My experience as a therapist involves many clients who deal with life's difficulties in courageous, loving, inspirational ways. I see clients who choose, out of religious values or for what they believe will be in the best interest of their children, to remain in a highly frustrating and unsatisfying marriage—and then proceed to make life work despite the marriage. I see clients who endure the death of a child, clients who are single parents working two jobs to make ends meet, clients who suffered but survived incredibly abusive childhoods—all quietly, unspectacularly going about living with purpose and dignity. It's like the national news reporting the destructive, insane events of the day—missing the more prevalent, but less sensational, every-day acts of people making life work.

Psychologically healthy people accept death but cherish life. They have little fear of death and they don't allow whatever fear of death they have to interfere with the time they have to live. They don't allow fear of any type to control or limit the range or quality of their life; they live and act despite whatever fear they have. They don't allow feelings to control what they do or don't do. Their craving for life makes self-concept irrelevant; their goal is to live each and every day with commitment and intensity. They enjoy life and are profoundly happy, whether or not life treats them kindly. They accept life on its terms rather than hope or demand that it be otherwise. They don't blame or regret the past, they don't fear the future—they value every present moment. Such people bring out the best in others. They accept other people as they are more than try to change them or insist that they be other than they are. They understand that there is no sensible way to respond to certain situations and behavior (that's what makes such situations and behavior crazy); but they always find sensible situations and sensible people to be part of their life. They think more about the family of man and the process of history than about just themselves and their biological family. They maintain a sense of tranquility, a sense of humor, a love for life and most everyone and everything. They live with zest and die in peace. Freud would never have speculated that they have a death instinct; their instinct for life is too obvious and too pervasive to allow such a conclusion.

On August 15, 2001 I was hit head-on by a truck whose driver lost control. In the fraction of a second between seeing the truck and the impact of the collision, I calmly realized that my life was over. The destruction and violence of the impending collision (see photo) was undeniable. There was no fear, no anger, no regret—only a totally peaceful awareness.

It was exactly as described by Eckhart Tolle:

> If you have ever been in a life-or-death emergency situation, you will know that it wasn't a problem. The mind didn't have time to fool around and make it into a problem. In a time of emergency, the mind stops; you become totally present in the Now, and something infinitely more powerful takes over…. In an emergency, either you survive or you don't. Either way, it is not a problem. [52]

Miraculously I survived—with only 2 broken ribs, a fractured sternum, and an assortment of contusions and abrasions. Every day since August 15 is an unearned gift of priceless value. Of course, so was every day before that fateful date.

This book is about life and the importance of appreciating the wonderful gift life is. Everything that I said in writing it seems even truer and more obvious since this miraculous extension of life. Happiness attains you when you surrender everything.

49 — Reprinted with the permission of Scribner, an imprint of Simon & Schuster Adult Publishing Group, from *On Death and Dying*, by Elizabeth Kubler-Ross, p. 276.

50 — *Constructive Living*, by David Reynolds (Honolulu: University of Hawaii Press, 1984), p. 70.

51 — *Don't Sweat the Small Stuff...and It's All Small Stuff*, by Richard Carlson (New York: Hyperion, 1997), pp. 59-60. Reprinted by permission of Hyperion.

52 — *The Power of Now: A Guide to Spiritual Enlightenment*, by Eckhart Tolle, p. 54. Used with permission from New World Library, Novato, CA, 94949. www.newworldlibrary.com

APPENDIX

WHAT YOU HAVE A RIGHT TO EXPECT
FROM A THERAPIST

Most clients have little knowledge regarding the qualifications of the person they see for therapy; they assume the therapist must be highly qualified or he wouldn't be in that position. I became aware of this when I worked in a clinic with a few psychologists (with a Doctoral Degree and therefore with the title "doctor") and many more social workers (with a Master's Degree and therefore not entitled "doctor"). Most of my clients who had previously seen a social worker referred to that therapist as""doctor;" they had no idea of the credentials of the person they had seen for treatment. I see clients who have no understanding of the difference between a psychologist and a psychiatrist; they expect I will prescribe medication and they assume a psychiatrist would be their best choice for marital therapy. They don't know whether the therapist they saw 5 years ago was a psychologist, psychiatrist, social worker, or of some other specialty or degree.

Of the various professionals you are likely to see when you go for mental health services, psychiatrists are highest in prestige. Psychiatrists are medical doctors—they complete medical school and then specialize in psychiatry. They make substantially more money than other mental health professionals. A few psychiatrists are psychoanalysts but almost none practice general psychotherapy. What psychiatrists are specialists in is medication; they primarily prescribe, and manage and monitor the use of, psychiatric medications. Like all mental health professionals, there are excellent psychiatrists and terrible psychiatrists. Many clients assume that psychiatrists, because they are medical doctors, are the most qualified for any and all mental health services. Psychiatrists have the most extensive training in medical and medication issues, but they are not the most qualified in areas beyond that specialization. Other mental health professionals have more extensive training in psychotherapy—the treatment of mental disorders through non-medical techniques.

Psychologists come next in prestige and pay. In most states to call oneself a psychologist a person needs a Doctoral Degree in psychology in addition to passing both a national and a state licensure examination. Psychologists have the title "doctor" not because of being physicians but because they have a Doctoral Degree—completing a 4 to 5-year program in courses relevant to therapy and human behavior. They have more training in these areas than any other mental health specialty. Psychologists are the only profession trained in psychological and neuropsychological testing—useful when the exact diagnosis or nature of the problem is unclear. Some psychologists are seeking prescription privileges for psychiatric medications. Their strongest argument is that primary care physicians, whose training and experience in this regard is limited, prescribe nearly 70% of these medications. My enthusiasm for this movement is lukewarm at best; in the ideal world, all psychiatric medications would be prescribed and monitored by psychiatrists—whose training in this regard is extensive.

Next in prestige are licensed social workers. They complete a 1 to 2-year Master's Degree program. Licensed social workers make ten to fifteen thousand dollars a year less than psychologists and thus have become increasingly popular in the cost conscious era of Managed Care. Most states have licensing laws and procedures for social workers; social workers who are licensed have titles such as "Licensed Independent Social Worker" (Ohio) or "Licensed Clinical Social Worker" (California). It's safe to assume someone using the title "Social Worker" (with no reference to "Licensed") is not licensed. Unlicensed social workers often have only a Bachelor's Degree and commonly work with community action programs or with governmental agencies such as Child Protective Services, Human Services, or Vocational Rehabilitation. If possible only see a social worker for psychotherapy who is licensed—or in the few states that do not have licensing for social workers, a social worker with a Master's Degree.

Marriage-Family-Therapists, particularly prevalent in California, have training roughly equivalent to that for social workers. The titles "counselor" and "therapist" need clarification, as they don't necessarily indicate therapeutic training or expertise. In some states almost anyone can call himself a "therapist" or a "counselor," with these titles merely indicating what the person does without reference to any specific degree or training. There are certified chemical dependency counselors and school counselors who have the appropriate training in those specific areas.

To make matters more complex, psychotherapy has less to do with training and more to do with individual ability. It is more a matter of art than science, more a matter of character than training. A social worker with a knack for therapy will serve your needs better than a psychologist who lacks therapeutic skill— even though the psychologist has more training. Regarding your best choice of who to see for therapy, see a psychiatrist if medication is your primary need or if you have extensive physical problems likely to require attention. Short of that, see a psychologist (in most states a psychologist can only use that title if he is licensed), a licensed social worker, or a Marriage-Family-Therapist —if possible, one who is recommended to you by someone who was pleased with his help.

The quality of psychiatric care has improved tremendously in the last few decades; not only have psychiatric medications improved, but more effective psychotherapeutic approaches have been developed and clarified for most psychiatric problems. Thirty years ago when clients went to see a therapist for Panic Disorder, for example, the therapist would talk with them ad nauseam about their childhood and current life situation, things that did little to nothing to alleviate the panic attacks. Today clients with Panic Disorder have a right to expect more from their therapist. Competent therapists know the medications that help with that disorder (and have access to a psychiatrist who can prescribe). They know that caffeine needs to be curtailed. They employ behavioral techniques (systematic desensitization, flooding, or other exposure techniques) that usually greatly reduce or even eliminate the panic attacks. The same can be said for most problems and conditions that people bring to therapy. You have a right to expect a therapist to know effective approaches for dealing with the problems you bring to him. There are, however, poor therapists just as there are poor mechanics, poor doctors and surgeons, poor teachers. Any consumer of mental health services owes it to himself to understand both the qualifications of his therapist and what he has a right to expect as part of competent treatment.

Other factors complicate this issue of what you have a right to expect from a therapist. Advances in medicine have led to the current tendency to view mental health problems (such as depression, anxiety, anger, drug or alcohol abuse) as medical problems—caused solely by genetics or chemical imbalance. This approach downplays, or even ignores, the role in these disorders of life circumstances and personality disturbance. Therapists who accept this view ignore important avenues for amelioration of these conditions and needlessly limit therapy to medication and offering sympathy and support.

In addition all therapists, myself included, in our graduate school programs were taught things about therapy that are wrong. These ideas became entrenched in the formative years of psychotherapy (as practiced not only by psychologists but the other mental health professions as described earlier in this appendix as well). Once ideas become entrenched, especially if they are more beliefs and opinions than objective facts that can be scientifically proven or disproved, they become difficult to uproot. If a therapist continues to believe and follow the faulty ideas he was taught, he will do you a disservice—providing less help than what otherwise might be possible.

These faulty concepts, in order of importance regarding the quality of care you are likely to receive, include:

1. Therapists should be nondirective rather than tell a client what is wrong and what can be done about that. They should wait for the client to discover for himself what's wrong and what to do about it.

2. Clients are fragile, weak, very vulnerable; you must handle them with extreme care.

3. The same therapeutic approach can be applied to all problems and all clients.

4. The goal of therapy is to produce the perfect psychological specimen.

5. Therapists shouldn't reveal anything about themselves or their personal life.

6. To inspire or motivate is not part of the therapist's role.

When I take my car for service, I expect the mechanic to figure out what's wrong with it, to know what to do to fix it (or refer me to someone who can), and to communicate those things to me so I can decide what to have done. Likewise, if I see an attorney regarding whether or not to file suit against a company for failure to deliver on a product they provided me, let's say paving my driveway, I expect the lawyer to let me know the legal facts for such a case, how good a case I have, what financial settlement I might expect if the suit is successful, how much the legal fees are likely to run, and what other legal options I have (such as Small Claims Court). In both cases I might seek a second opinion; but after I have been given the advice of those I consult, I need to decide what to do.

When you see a therapist, you have a right to expect the same. You should expect a therapist, with your help, to clarify your problems and the treatment options for those problems. Unfortunately clients too frequently discontinue therapy because their therapist never clarified their problems or the treatment approaches for those problems. Some therapists take pride in operating this way (as they were taught in graduate school), despite its total lack of common sense. There's too much truth to the joke about psychoanalysis where the person has been going for analysis three times a week for 2 years. After endless free association without any feedback, he can't stand it any longer. So he says, "Doc, I need to know, have I made any progress; am I at least on the right track?" The doctor answers, "No comprendo Ingles." Some therapists believe offering feedback and advice is unprofessional; in reality not doing that is unprofessional and a failure to meet the goals that motivate clients to come for therapy—help in being able to live more productively and with greater satisfaction.

In medicine, and many other specializations, there is the issue of informed consent. Your physician is an expert in the field of medicine—but that doesn't give him the right to force you to take a particular medication or to undergo a particular surgical procedure. Your physician, however, is legally obligated to diagnose your condition and to inform you of the various treatment approaches for your condition and the likely outcome of each. Provided with that information, you then have the right and the responsibility to decide what to do (it's your body). You have this same right to informed consent in psychotherapy; unfortunately some therapists confuse your right to disregard their opinions and advice as an excuse for not providing those opinions and advice.

Based upon my training and years of clinical practice, I know more than most clients about the situational and psychological problems that arise and interfere with a person's life, and how to deal effectively with those problems. I tell clients what diagnoses I give them and what I can do to help them improve those conditions. For example, I might inform a particular client that he is suffering from both Major Depression (listing the symptoms of that disorder) and Avoidant Personality Disorder (again listing those symptoms) and that I think he needs to learn to become more assertive and to care less about what others think about him. I would let him know that all experts advise the use of an antidepressant for Major Depression and why. I would inform him of the psychotherapy approaches I recommend for his depression, his Avoidant Personality Disorder, and his problems with assertiveness and excessively needing other's approval. The choice is then up to him regarding how he wants to proceed. I inform anxiety clients how to best deal with their anxiety disorder. I inform marital couples what the most recent research indicates regarding how to make their marriage work. I offer my clients everything I know out of my expertise because that is my responsibility; I owe them that. But I let them know this is merely my well-informed opinion; they need ultimately to make their own decisions. They can't and shouldn't do something just because I think they should—they can only consider the source of the advice; just as they shouldn't do something just because their minister, spouse, neighbor, mother, or most of Western Civilization thinks they should.

Therapists have been taught to be cautious in what they do with clients; this approach is based on the belief that people in therapy are fragile and the wrong suggestion, or even the truth about their mental health problems, could be catastrophic (pushing them over the edge into a nervous breakdown or even suicide). This is the wrong approach and does disservice to the client. This approach treats clients as if they were infants and is an insult to them. The attitude is similar to that expressed by Jack Nicholson in the movie *A Few Good Men* when he tells the investigating officer, "You can't handle the truth." Just as you have a right to know what problems the therapist thinks you have (you're not so fragile you can't handle that), you also have a right to expect your therapist to take a dynamic approach in trying to resolve those problems. The worst thing a therapist can do is nothing at all. You have a right to expect your therapist to take an active role in leading you to a solution of the problems that brought you to therapy. A therapist who asks endless questions, who never leads to decisions and a resolution of problems, is doing you an injustice. Good therapists offer possible solutions; if one solution is unacceptable or doesn't work, they look for another. They are experts: they suggest alternatives you never considered, knowledge you didn't have, advice you wouldn't get from your next-door neighbor.

Some therapists are reluctant to let the client see his record; few if any clients are so fragile that this would cause irreparable psychological damage.

Paranoid clients might be an exception but even then I don't think so. They will reject your notion that they are paranoid but I think it's still best to share that opinion; maybe they will leave you for another therapist but you were never going to be able to help them anyway. Some clients do go therapist shopping; if you tell them something they don't want to hear (like the husband-attacking woman I mentioned in Chapter Five), they may look for another therapist. But that is not as bad as failing to be truthful regarding what you think regarding their problems and what they need.

You have the right to expect a therapist to be flexible and to be able to use a wide range of approaches depending on both the problem and you the client. Flexibility, as I mentioned in Chapter Four, is essential for mental health; certainly you have a right to expect a therapist to be flexible. I'm skeptical of the therapist who uses the same therapeutic approach in all cases—whether it's psychoanalysis, hypnosis, psychodrama, relaxation techniques, cognitive therapy, or whatever. Therapists should know a wide range of therapeutic approaches and techniques and be able to choose the most appropriate technique or combination of techniques for the problem at hand—rather than using the only approach and technique they know or are comfortable with. Effective therapists use a wide range of techniques to help their clients develop greater choice regarding what they are able to do and what they are able to avoid doing. By way of analogy, I offer the story of the young doctor just out of medical school who goes into practice with a doctor nearing retirement. One day a woman runs out of the older doctor's office screaming, "I can't be pregnant, I can't be pregnant;"

and then runs hysterically out of their suite. The younger doctor is bothered by this and asks the older doctor, "How could you tell a 65-year-old woman she's pregnant and upset her like that?" The older doctor comments, "Well, it sure cured her hiccups."

Another issue that makes the picture less clear is there has been some change regarding the goal of therapy. The established goal of therapy in bygone days was reflected in the statement "The unexamined life isn't worth living," meaning the most important thing in life is to understand the factors that influence us in the process of life. The modern goal of therapy is better reflected in the statement "The unlived life is worth examining," meaning the most important thing is to live; the only need for therapy is when and if a person becomes blocked in that process. I won't concern myself about a flaw my client has as long as that flaw isn't causing significant dysfunction in the client's life. I'm not trying to produce a person without flaws, which is impossible and would take forever; I'm trying to produce a person who can live life in all its important aspects. It isn't the goal of therapy to produce the perfect psychological specimen.

When I take my car for an oil change, I don't expect my mechanic to fix everything wrong with my car; although I do expect him to let me know if he discovers some serious problem I might not be aware of. When I see my physician because I have the flu, I don't expect him to do a complete physical; although again I do expect him to let me know about a problem he suspects that could be more serious than the flu that brought me in. The same holds true for psychotherapy. If a client sees me for panic attacks, I won't set about doing marital therapy or trying to help the client become more assertive (even though these might be problems he has). I will bring those issues up only if treating them is necessary for the successful treatment of his panic attacks or if they seem to be causing major problems in his life.

In the old view of therapy, therapists never revealed anything about their personal life; the idea was the therapist shouldn't influence his client's choices or decisions because that might be biased by the therapist's limited views, values, and beliefs. My view, held by many therapists even if we are the minority, is that therapists should offer things from their personal life that are relevant and helpful; yet not dump on the client their personal problems or information about their life that serves no purpose regarding the problems that brought the client to therapy. I reject the view that a client should spill his guts to me, tell me the most intimate details of his life, and that I should steadfastly refuse to reveal anything about my life and myself. I reveal things about myself when I judge it will be helpful to the client; I don't reveal personal things when I don't think that information will serve the client any purpose. If a client tells me he is being downsized, and I was downsized (as I was), I reveal what I learned from that experience and what was helpful to me in dealing with it.

Many therapists were taught to avoid presenting a positive view of life. It was viewed as unprofessional and an intrusion on the client's life to suggest to him that life is a neat opportunity rather than something to be feared or endured reluctantly. This is nonsense. Motivation and inspiration is an inherent part of the therapist's role. Many clients who come for therapy have lost belief in life and/or belief in themselves. Such clients need more than mere therapeutic technique.

A therapist who is incapable of or unwilling to inspire and motivate clients should not be in practice.

Another issue is whether you should see a male or female therapist. In most instances this should not be an issue of concern; for specific therapeutic issues it might. Many people being seen for sexual issues prefer to see a therapist of the same sex. A woman working on her relationship with a daughter might prefer to see a female therapist. Ironically, if an important issue in your life is comfortableness with the opposite sex, my advice would be to see a therapist of the opposite sex. You might be more comfortable seeing a same sex therapist, but seeing an opposite sex therapist has greater potential for therapeutic gain.

The above issue presents in parallel forms. Christian clients sometimes seek a Christian therapist. There is currently an impetus to train more Hispanic therapists to serve America's growing Hispanic population. Similar issues exist regarding any ethnic group, any sexual orientation, any age group. Alcohol treatment programs have struggled over the relative importance of therapists in recovery (ex-alcoholics) versus therapists of high academic training. Seeing a therapist of your own gender or subculture is a good idea when therapy specifically involves those issues: male or female sexuality, mother-daughter relation-ships, reconciling one's religious principles with divorce, functioning in a healthy manner in the gay community. My bias is to discount these factors unless such specific cultural factors will be the focus of therapy. A lesbian client would do well to see an excellent lesbian therapist, or an excellent therapist with extensive training and experience with this population; but she would do better to see an excellent heterosexual therapist than a mediocre lesbian therapist—unless the focus of therapy is specifically lesbian issues. Most importantly, I encourage anyone to discontinue seeing a therapist who doesn't understand and accept him and relate to him as the person he is.

In selecting a therapist, I personally would be more concerned about technical knowledge, practice patterns, and psychological health than about age, gender, religious beliefs, sexual orientation, or ethnicity and culture. Just as it makes sense to avoid the mechanic whose car runs poorly, it makes sense to avoid the therapist who isn't psychologically healthy. I would look for a therapist with a love and zest for life; a sense of humor; more tranquility and less anger, depression, or anxiety; a grandiose love of self combined with profound humility; general flexibility; and the ability to like and accept other people as they are. His superior knowledge of mental health issues compared to yours shouldn't result in an attitude of being superior to you. Rather than playing "the doctor role" and forcing you into "the patient role," he should promote an atmosphere of teamwork based upon mutual respect. It shouldn't take more than a couple of therapy sessions to become aware of how well a therapist meets these criteria.

Another way of looking at this issue is what I have a right to expect from my clients. I expect my marital couples to be interested in solving their marital problems, rather than to remain stuck forever in blaming and attacking their partner. I expect my individual clients to move beyond endless complaining. It's exhausting to deal with clients who refuse to work toward a resolution of their problems. Maybe that's okay with them; it's not okay with me. Life is too valuable to waste time accomplishing nothing. I will go to endless lengths to help a client resolve his problems; no amount of money would motivate me to tolerate a client who only wants to use me to complain about how miserable life is. When I find myself becoming bored in a therapy session, it likely means no real therapy is going on—due either to the lack of motivation or knowledge on the part of my client, myself, or both.

A practical guideline for when to seek the help of a mental health professional is whenever you find yourself stuck in some important area or aspect of life, unable to resolve the situation using your own knowledge and resources. Once you have decided to take that step, seek a therapist with the appropriate credentials who (presented in their order of importance):

1. Takes a dynamic approach in helping you clarify and resolve your problems, including suggesting and explaining specific treatment approaches.

2. Functions in a practical, time-efficient manner because time is better spent living than in therapy.

3. Relates in a warm personal way rather than being distant, aloof, "professionally impersonal."

4. Respects your strengths and abilities rather than seeing you as fragile and help-less and as inferior to him.

5. Exudes a belief in life and the importance of making life work.

6. Exemplifies psychological health.

7. Understands and accepts you and relates to you as the person you are.

8. Is flexible enough to adjust to you rather than insisting that you adjust to him and his rigid style of practice.

I conclude this appendix with one observation about Managed Care as it relates specifically to mental health services (I have worked with the same national Managed Care organization since 1979—first in Southern California, then in Ohio, and now in Northern California). Almost by accident, Managed Care has provided an invaluable asset to mental health treatment by pushing for practical time-effective methods for dealing with clients and their problems. The motivation of these organizations has been to save money; but it has provided clients with something they had a right to expect all along—practical, effective, time-efficient care. Too often in the past, therapists acted as if they had all the time in the world. Maybe they do; you don't.

RECOMMENDED READING

Bourne, Edmund. *The Anxiety and Phobia Workbook*, Third Edition. Oakland: New Harbinger Publications, 2001

Burns, David. *Ten Days to Self-Esteem*. New York: William Morrow and Company, 1993

Burns, David. *Feeling Good: The New Mood Therapy*, Revised and Updated Version. New York: Avon Books, 1999

Carlson, Richard. *Don't Sweat the Small Stuff...and It's All Small Stuff*. New York: Hyperion, 1997

Chodron, Pema. *When Things Fall Apart*. Boston: Shambhala Library, 2000

Dyer, Wayne. *Your Erroneous Zones*. New York: Avon Books, 1977

Ellis, Albert. *Feeling Better, Getting Better, Staying Better*. Atascadero, California: Impact Publishers, 2001

Ellis, Albert and Robert Harper. *A Guide to Rational Living*, Third Edition. Hollywood: Melvin Powers Wilshire Book Company, 1997

Gottman, John. *Why Marriages Succeed or Fail*. New York: Simon & Schuster, 1994

Gottman, John. *The Seven Principles for Making Marriage Work*. New York: Three Rivers Press, 1999

Kubler-Ross, Elizabeth. *On Death and Dying*. New York: Scribner, 1997

Kushner, Harold. *When Bad Things Happen to Good People*. New York: Schocken Books, 1981

Lerner, Harriet. *The Dance of Anger*. New York: Harper & Row, 1985

Mandino, Og. *The Greatest Miracle in the World*. New York: Bantam Books, 1975

McGraw, Phillip. *Self Matters*. New York: Simon & Schuster Source, 2001

McKay, Matthew, Rogers, Peter and Judith McKay. *When Anger Hurts*. Oakland: New Harbinger Publications, 1989

McKay, Matthew and Patrick Fanning. *Self-Esteem*, Third Edition. Oakland: New Harbinger Publications, 2000

Millman, Dan. *The Way of the Peaceful Warrior*. Novato, California: New World Library, 2000

Reynolds, David. *Constructive Living*. Honolulu: University of Hawaii Press, 1984

Tolle, Eckhart. *The Power of Now: A Guide to Spiritual Enlightenment*. Novato, California: New World Library, 1999

BIBLIOGRAPHY

Bandler, Richard and John Grinder. *Reframing*. Moab, Utah: Real People Press, 1982.

Benson, Herbert. *The Relaxation Response*. New York: Morrow, 1975.

Bourne, Edmund. *The Anxiety and Phobia Workbook*, Third Edition. Oakland: New Harbinger Publications, 2001

Burns, David. *Ten Days to Self-Esteem*. New York: William Morrow and Company, 1993

Burns, David. *Feeling Good: The New Mood Therapy*, Revised and Updated Version. New York: Avon Books, 1999

Carlson, Richard. *Don't Sweat the Small Stuff...and It's All Small Stuff*. New York: Hyperion, 1997

Dyer, Wayne. *Your Erroneous Zones*. New York: Avon Books, 1977

Ellis, Albert. *Feeling Better, Getting Better, Staying Better*. Atascadero, California: Impact Publishers, 2001

Ellis, Albert and Robert Harper. *A Guide to Rational Living*, Third Edition. Hollywood: Melvin Powers Wilshire Book Company, 1997

Erickson, Milton and Ernest Rossi. *Varieties of double bind*. The American Journal of Clinical Hypnosis, 1975, 17(3), 143-157

Gottman, John. *Why Marriages Succeed or Fail.* New York: Simon & Schuster, 1994

Gottman, John. *The Seven Principles for Making Marriage Work.* New York: Three Rivers Press, 1999

Hesse, Herman. *Siddhartha.* New York: New Directions, 1951

Horney, Karen. *Neurosis and Human Growth: The Struggle toward Self-Realization.* New York: W. W. Norton & Company, 1950

Kubler-Ross, Elizabeth. *On Death and Dying.* New York: Scribner, 1997

Kushner, Harold. *When Bad Things Happen to Good People.* New York: Schocken Books, 1981

Lerner, Harriet. *The Dance of Anger.* New York: Harper & Row, 1985

Mandino, Og. *The Greatest Miracle in the World.* New York: Bantam Books, 1975

McKay, Matthew, Rogers, Peter and Judith McKay. *When Anger Hurts.* Oakland: New Harbinger Publications, 1989

McKay, Matthew and Patrick Fanning. *Self-Esteem*, Third Edition. Oakland: New Harbinger Publications, 2000

Millman, Dan. *The Warrior Athlete.* Walpole, New Hampshire: Stillpoint Publishing, 1979

Millman, Dan. *The Way of the Peaceful Warrior.* Novato, California: New World Library, 2000

Millman, Dan. *Everyday Enlightenment: The Twelve Gateways to Personal Growth.* New York: Warner Books, 1998

Reynolds, David. *Constructive Living.* Honolulu: University of Hawaii Press, 1984

Shah, Idries. *Tales of the Dervishes.* London: Octagon Press, 1982

Shah, Idries. *The Pleasantries of the Incredible Mulla Nasrudin.* London: Octagon Press, 1983

Tolle, Eckhart. *The Power of Now: A Guide to Spiritual Enlightenment.* Novato, California: New World Library, 1999

Zeig, Jeffrey (Editor). *A Teaching Seminar with Milton H. Erickson.* New York: Brunner/Mazel Publishers, 1980

www.drzinkle.com